Scratching the Woodchuck

SCRATCHING
THE
WOODCHUCK

Nature on an Amish Farm

DAVID KLINE

DRAWINGS BY WENDELL MINOR

The University of Georgia Press

ATHENS AND LONDON

University of Georgia Press paperback edition, 1999
Published by the University of Georgia Press
Athens, Georgia 30602
© 1997 by David Kline
All rights reserved
Drawings © 1997 by Wendell Minor
Book design by Wendell Minor and Sandra Hudson
Set in Monotype Walbaum with Bodoni Swash display

The paper in this book meets the guidelines for
permanence and durability of the Committee on
Production Guidelines for Book Longevity
of the Council on Library Resources.
Printed in the United States of America
03 02 01 00 99   P   5 4 3 2 1

*The Library of Congress has cataloged the cloth edition
of this book as follows:*
Library of Congress Cataloging in Publication Data
Kline, David.
Scratching the woodchuck : nature on an
Amish farm / David Kline.
p.   cm.
ISBN 0-8203-1938-4 (alk. paper)
1. Natural history—Ohio. 2. Farm life—Ohio. 3. Kline, David.
I. Title.
QH105.03K56   1997
577.5'5'09771—dc21   97-8221

ISBN 0-8203-2154-0 (pbk. : alk. paper)

British Library Cataloging in Publication Data available

To my friends,

who have walked with me

CONTENTS

ACKNOWLEDGMENTS

I am grateful to many people for their help with this book. First, to my family for their patience when I had deadlines looming and, especially, to my wife, Elsie, for her sharp eye in reining in grammatical errors.

To Scott Savage, friend and editor of *Plain*. He has been a source of inspiration to me, and the visits with Scott and Mary Ann and their children are special occasions for us.

To Melody Snure, managing editor of the *Daily Record* in Wooster, Ohio, who previously published some of the material in this book. I am forever grateful for her generosity.

To the editorial staff of *Family Life*, who helped with the birth of some of the essays collected here.

Barbara Ras, my editor, deserves great thanks for nurturing this book, for creating order out of chaos, for her endless enthusiasm, and for her gentleness in reminding me of urgent deadlines.

INTRODUCTION

I grew up on the farm where I now live with my wife and children. The farm rests at that edge where the gently rolling hills of the Allegheny plateau begin to flatten out into the table land of northwestern Ohio; where the eastern hardwoods begin to give way to the cottonwoods and burr oaks and prairie lands; where joe-pye weed meets black-eyed Susan. From here to the southeast, hill country extends to the Atlantic coastal plain and, beginning twenty miles to the northwest, flat land reaches all the way to the foothills of the Rockies.

Of course, when I was growing up there were no coastal plains or Rockies, at least not until fifth-grade geography. My world consisted of farmlands in a radius of about four miles from home—a distance that could be walked or biked in several hours.

In that circle were perhaps fifty farms with a variety of livestock and a patchwork of fields, two villages, and several country schools. One of these, Elm Grove, a one-room public school, so named but shaded by a massive white oak, was eight-tenths of a mile south and half a mile west of our farm. A walk that could take anywhere from fifteen minutes to two hours, depending on the weather and the season. It was here at Elm Grove, surrounded by rich fields and woodlands and within a quarter mile of an interesting bog, that I spent eight glorious school years and where my love for nature was nurtured.

My teacher for seven of those years, for grades two through eight, was Clarence F. Zuercher, the finest naturalist I have ever met. Interestingly, Mr. Zuercher had also been my father's teacher for the second through the eighth grades, forty years before in another part of the county. My interest in nature was planted before I entered school, but under Mr. Zuercher's tutelage it sprouted and grew.

Mr. Zuercher, the son of Swiss immigrants, had a broad knowledge of the natural world, and he immersed us in the flora and fauna of the local watershed from September through May. From birds and reptiles to trees and wildflowers to butterflies and moths, nothing escaped his sharp eyes. We learned to identify all the species of local trees not only by the shape of their leaves but also by the look and texture of their bark and by their fruits. Mr. Zuercher also had a keen interest in the fishes of the local waterways.

A creek, the Salt, ran from southeast to northwest about a mile north of the schoolhouse. It meandered for half a mile across the western end of our pasture field. The creek was spring fed, clear, and fast flowing, dropping ten feet per mile, but it harbored many deep and mysterious pools that made superb fishing and swimming holes.

Oftentimes in early April our teacher would dismiss school half an hour early. In his '52 Ford he headed for the creek to fish for black suckers. And he was an expert at it. He elevated sucker fishing to an art.

One spring he took three of us boys along to try our luck at sucker fishing. Since the schoolhouse was at the outer edge of the Killbuck watershed, Mr. Zuercher traveled several miles downstream where the creek was wider and deeper and even more alluring than it was on our farm. Even the snakes were bigger. Our communication was by gesture and whisper. He scoffed at expensive tackle and fished with a cane pole. While we tried our best, and caught a few, he kept hauling them in.

We were in the presence of a master fisherman who understood fish as well as he did the shenanigans of schoolboys.

While we were fishing he pointed out a soaring red-tailed hawk overhead and nesting kingfishers in a streambank burrow nearby. Also, a yellow warbler in an old willow. Soon choretime came, and we had to leave because Mr. Zuercher, besides being a teacher and fisherman and naturalist, was also a farmer. The cows had to be milked.

When I was ten years old, spring on the farm did not begin with the fieldwork; it began with sucker fishing in that wonderful creek. That could be anywhere from late March through mid-April when the black suckers began actively feeding.

To us, sucker fishing was stealth fishing, unlike the carefree bobber fishing for rock bass and bluegill later in the spring and in the clockless summer. One had to tread softly on the creek bank lest the wary fish would detect your footfall, hide in the tangles of underwater tree roots, and refuse to take your bait, no matter how enticingly the earthworm wiggled in front of their downturned mouths.

It took skill to catch suckers in the clear and cold waters of early spring, when the single track of the freshwater mussel showed as plainly on the unmarked sand of the creek bottom as a white chalk mark on a clean blackboard. If the fish weren't spooked, they would start at the head of the earthworm and slowly suck it up. When the line began moving toward the deep dark mysterious root-tangled part of the hole, where the sunning water snakes had dropped into only minutes before, and goose bumps of anticipation crept up your arm, you set the hook and hauled the resisting fish to the bank. The suckers had tough sinewy mouths, and once they were hooked they stayed hooked. Bass would sometimes shake loose the hook, and we made diving leaps to grab a flopping fish before it regained the safety of the water, where it surely wouldn't take a bait again. On good days several dozen suckers could be caught.

As the water warmed, the suckers seemed to disappear, and our attention turned to rock bass and bluegill and horned chubs. These were less wary fish, and fishing for them was more carefree. We could slosh bare feet in the water, and the fish kept on biting. The season of summer officially arrived, not on the summer solstice, but when the water became warm enough for swimming. That occurred sometime in early June, when the water snakes began shying away from the heat of midday and sought shade instead. Along with the heat of the season came hay making and small-grain harvest—threshing time—which meant more work for us and less time for woods and creek snooping.

At the end of three months of summer vacation and after harvest, we could hardly wait for school to begin in early September. Most of us were at the schoolhouse on opening morning long before Mr. Zuercher arrived a little before 8:30 and unlocked the door. We scrambled over the newly oiled wood floor to find choice desks near windows of the back door or next to the tanned skin of the red fox; we unpacked our pencils and other school necessities and fled for the ball diamond for ten minutes of play before the bell rang. Regardless of where we settled, Mr. Zuercher moved each of us a desk forward every month.

But he never let the classroom interfere with our education. I can't recall my class ever getting through a textbook before the school year ended in late May. At that time every eighth-grade student had to pass a state exam in order to graduate. When my class was in the eighth grade and preparing for that dreaded test of two hundred questions, Mr. Zuercher told us that he didn't have much time to devote to us, but that we should read, read, and read. He would send us out to his car so that we could study uninterrupted by the other classes, and one dog, sharing the single room. Of course, he sent the keys along so that we could listen to the radio. Usually, Elizabeth, the only girl in our class, would have the front seat, and so naturally we boys endured the country music she preferred. We thought it was silly that every mournful singer either lost his dog or his car or his girlfriend.

Mr. Zuercher believed that all of nature was part of the web of life. From the delicate maidenhair fern and reptiles to the birds of prey and hordes of insects that shared our farms. He insisted that each filled an important niche in the rich diversity of life and he taught us to tread lightly on the land. "Give more back than you take," he said. "And don't pay too much attention to the agricultural experts," he cautioned us. Since all of his forty-five or so students in the eight grades were from farms, we took his advice seriously.

From Mr. Zuercher I learned to see the natural world as a boundless adventure. There was no end to the discoveries and beauty to be found beneath rocks, in the creek, in the woods, in the sky, and in humans. (When a student gazing out one of the windows spotted a Goodyear blimp, classes were dismissed, and everybody went outside to watch the huge airship crawl through the sky as slowly as a snail crossing a road. The daydreaming student was praised for his keen sense of observation.)

One of the reasons I immersed myself in nature was that throughout my eight years in that one-room school, I stuttered. Severely enough that I had a constant gut-gnawing fear of speaking in front of my class. In the woods I had no such fears—the trees and flowers and birds and moths and butterflies and frogs and snakes and clouds and stars never laughed at me. To me, the God that created all that beauty and grace must be a wonderful and loving Being. Nature became a sanctuary, a solace, for me. A realm of limitless love.

Perhaps my fear of speech during my adolescent years turned me to writing. I became fascinated by words that I could write or read but could never utter in front of people. To the trees and wild creatures, yes, but never to humans. Those twenty-six letters of the alphabet above the blackboard intrigued me. So did the dictionary. There were infinite ways, I thought, to arrange words to describe the boundless beauty and mystery beyond the doorstep.

Sometime during those formative years in grade school I began keeping a daily diary. The daily entries were short, often a terse "Went to school"; "Played ball and walked to the woods"; "Saw a sparrow hawk kill a cardinal"; "Had our Christmas program. Levi was Scrooge. My gift: a pocketknife and a flashlight."

It wasn't until I was drafted in the mid-sixties, in my late teens, and worked in a Cleveland hospital, that I began serious journal writing. Page after page of human activities. There seemed to be a dearth of nature in the city, at least when compared with the country. But then I had access to a telephone, and so I called the Audubon Rare Bird Alert almost daily to find out whether there were any jaegers or rare gulls hanging out along the lakeshore. Or perhaps a snowy owl at Burke Lakefront Airport, or a Townsend's solitaire at a city birdfeeder. These rare birds and some common chickadees and the spring's first dandelions, and of course, the city's fine snowstorms, found their way into my journal.

When I moved to the city I looked forward to the change of scenery, the throb of humanity, easy access to a well-stocked library, and by not having those morning and evening barn chores, time to read. But I wasn't prepared for the cultural shock that followed. While the sounds in the country tend to be soft, muted, and musical, city sounds were harsh: tires squealing, shouts in the night, and a constant wailing of sirens. Someone injured, dying, a fire, a stabbing—which meant work for me in the hospital. I could help those unfortunate victims of the city.

Another part of the city life I found bewildering at first was how people constantly complained about the weather. It was either too hot or too cold or too wet. Even if it was extremely dry and the crops and gardens desperately needed moisture, the weatherman would say that the weekend would be miserable because of the threat of rain. For me, coming from a culture that was so closely tied to the land and the weather and the rhythms of the seasons, their attitudes were absurd.

At home no one complained about the weather. After all, God controlled everything, the sun, the clouds, the wind, and the rain. Complaining was finding fault with God, we were told. My dad would tell the tragic story of his Swiss immigrant neighbor who cursed the weather. One early summer day while Charlie was cultivating corn a thunderstorm came up. He sought shelter in the chicken house. Maybe he shook his fist at the sky as he sometimes did. In any event, lightning struck the building and Charlie died.

In time I settled into city life. I found my way to the public library, visited the museums, attended different churches, and went downtown to sit on park benches and to watch people. They were always in a hurry, head down, briefcase in hand, rushing everywhere. Never had I felt more alone, sitting on those cold steel park benches, even though I was surrounded by people.

Part of the difference between city and country was that in the country we tend to see God in every aspect of creation. Likely because most of the things in our lives are God-created: the grass, the trees, the birds and mammals, and the people. In the city so much is human-created: concrete, asphalt, glass, steel on rubber, industrial smoke, and those ugly tangles of overhead electrical wires. Why, I thought, if you could live in the country, would anyone choose to live in the city?

I found out that in the city, even more than in the country, where many houses are never locked, the home became a sanctuary. A place, once the dead bolts were secured, where one went to escape that "out there"; where family and friends assembled within the security of one another. It was in the homes where I learned that urban people are very much like rural people—they care, laugh, and worship the same God. Maybe not the omnipresent God of my rural community, but the same one nevertheless. And I found out that there are angels in the city.

I moved to Cleveland in late November, and when I was returning after spending the Christmas holiday at home, the Greyhound bus got caught in one of the early winter snowstorms northeastern Ohio is famous for. Arriving three hours late, in the early morning hours, the city was at a standstill. The city buses, my usual mode of travel to my apartment eight miles out in a suburb (for thirty-five cents), had quit for the night, and there were no taxis running. The city was asleep.

Since I did not have enough money for a hotel room and sleeping in the bus station wasn't an option, I walked into the howling fury of the storm. Almost immediately car lights came out of the swirling snow and stopped by the curb; the driver reached over and opened the passenger door.

"Do you need help, or a ride?" a voice asked.

"Indeed I do, but I have almost no money," I said.

After the driver said it was no problem, I got in the car, and we headed, alone on the wide streets, for my new home. The driver, an African American with some gray in his hair, said he had woken at 1:00 A.M. and hearing the storm outside could not go back to sleep. He thought someone might be needing help, so he got in his car and drove to the bus station.

Finally, after numerous U-turns on the slippery roads, we reached the street where I lived. He did not want to take any money for the ride, but I insisted and gave him all I had. As I watched the tail lights of his car fade into the storm, my eyes welled with tears of gratitude for this angel of mercy.

That man forever changed my view of the city. I realized that love can live in the human heart anywhere. I knew that the Good Samaritan was alive and well.

When my work in the city was finished, I came back to my boyhood home, to the farm, and discovered that the quietude bothered me. But it did not take long to recover and rediscover the beauty and the pleasures of nature on the farm.

When I walked to the barn in the early morning, bright and lovely Venus was there in the eastern sky to greet me, instead of being lost in the haze of a city's light pollution. And when I plowed again in early spring, I watched a kestrel "rung upon the rein of a wimpling wing" hover above a meadow vole, and then swiftly drop, talons flared, for a meal. I was reunited to the natural world and retuned to the natural rhythms of the seasons—the memory of the land came rushing back.

I could look at the farm and its inhabitants through the eyes of a stranger and began to see things I had missed before. Didn't Emerson write that a man standing in his own field is unable to see it? Before my return I had never seen the courtship flight of the horned lark, so common yet so elusive, in our fields. This past spring, as I have in many springs past, I watched the male lark perform his rite of spring. I was planting corn when he took flight from the tilled field. Singing and circling until he was five hundred feet above the team and me, the lark serenaded his mate, and us, for fifteen minutes before dropping back to earth.

On my homecoming to the farm, every tree, every bird, every flower, every insect, was just as vivid and interesting and mysterious as it was during those days at the one-room school. Of course, by that time, every one-room public school in Ohio was forced by the State Board of Education to close its doors. The antiquated system wasn't providing an adequate education for its students, the board proclaimed. Our school district had seven schools, which had their last classes and nature walks in 1960; they were then consolidated into one school. For the first time the school district had to buy buses, and within a few years our small district was gobbled up by a larger district: that typical scenario of a small fish being swallowed by a bigger one and so on down the line. But as Bill KcKibben said, "Bigger means only bigger, it doesn't mean better."

As far as literature goes, my passion for nature was probably more stirred by those pocket-sized Golden Nature Guides that our teacher kept on hand than any other book. He had four—trees, wildflowers, butterflies and moths, and birds. In the late 1950s our county bought a bookmobile, "The Travelling Bookshelf," which then made its rounds to the rural schools every six weeks. Then, my natural history reading expanded dramatically and included Jack London, Thornton Burgess, and Edwin Way Teale. It wasn't, however, until I returned from the city that I "discovered" the writings of Aldo

Leopold, Hal Borland, John Hay, Wendell Berry, and countless other great writers.

I continued to write in my journals about nature on the farm and eventually sort of fell into writing for publication. A friend loaned me a book, *Communicating the Outdoor Experience*. Even though the book was intended for rod and gun writers, it taught me a great deal on how to write for publication.

The last time I visited Mr. Zuercher, he was in his eighties and housebound for the first time in his life. He told me in a voice reduced to a whisper by the ravages of Parkinson's disease, "Nature is so interesting. You are never too old to enjoy it. I never went on a walk that I didn't see or find something exciting and interesting. In Proverbs we read that 'It is the glory of God to conceal things, but it is our glory to search things out.' Over the years I have searched out many things." Then he smiled.

THE FARMSTEAD

MOLES

One night last week one of our cats killed a mole and, after it tired of playing with its prize, left it uneaten on the barn floor. (Moles have an offensive taste and are almost never eaten by cats.) I examined the down-on-his-luck creature and, as I always do on finding a mole, marveled at the beauty of its fur. This one's pelage was dark gray, nearly black, soft and dense. Mole fur has no definite "lay" to it. It can be brushed forward or backward, up or down, and it lies naturally flat. This serves the burrowing animal well: when backing up in its tight tunnel, the mole never gets its fur rubbed the wrong way.

This mole must have left its subterranean home during the thaw. Maybe its tunnel filled with meltwater, and on exiting it was surprised by the cat. My guess, though, is that it wasn't floodwater that drove the nearly blind animal to the surface, but the call of the February-through-April mole mating season.

This is the only time of the year that moles venture above ground frequently and fall victim to predators. As long as they stay in their subsurface labyrinth of burrows, moles live fairly secure lives. Shrews are the only visitors to the underground runways, but they pose no threat to adult moles.

The six-inch-long eastern mole (*Scalopus aquaticus*), the most common and widespread species in the eastern United States, is ideally equipped for digging. It lacks a neck, and its head has no visible ears or eyes; it thus gives the appearance of an oblong beanbag with a tail on one end and a snout on the other. The mole's oversized, clawlike front teeth are placed well forward on the snout end, and its palms face to the sides, awkward for walking but efficient for digging.

When the mole digs those annoying tunnels through lawns, it does so by using its front feet with a breaststroke motion. If the ground is mellow, the mole can dig without moving much soil; it simply forces its way through by raising the sod. Tunneling in daylight is sometimes the mole's waterloo if the lawn owner or gardener spies the rising sod at the end of a mole tunnel and has a garden spade in hand. Even without external ears, though, moles are extremely sensitive to ground vibrations and will "vanish" as soon as they feel the irate spade-wielder's footfall. One has to use stealth to catch a mole.

Besides the eastern mole in our yard, we occasionally find the star-nosed mole. This interesting digger is the size of the eastern mole, but sports a longer tail and, instead of a pointy noise, has a fleshy sunburst on the end of its snout. Twenty-two pink tentacles circle the mole's proboscis. This mole is the only animal in the world with a star nose—a world-class schnauzer.

Moles are almost exclusively carnivorous and may eat half their weight daily in earthworms, soil insects, and grubs. Flowing through soil takes a great amount of energy. Sometimes a mole will follow a row of newly sprouted corn and eat every kernel for fifteen to twenty feet. Their primary food, however, is earthworms. In a healthy lawn where earthworms flourish, there are bound to be moles.

In winter, moles follow the earthworms below the frostline by digging deep-running tunnels. It is when excavating these deep, permanent burrows that the moles bring soil to the surface and create those exasperating molehills so common in spring lawns. Earlier this winter the moles were active in our lawn under the snow. When the snow melted during the January thaw, there were molehills everywhere. They must have created an entire new mole city. Perhaps the energetic earth movers are developing a mole mall.

The winter habits of moles are not well known, except that they don't hibernate. Sometime in late April or May, in an underground nest of dried grass and leaves, the female mole will give birth to three to five young. Born pink and hairless, the young moles grow rapidly, and in a month they are ready to go earthworm hunting on their own.

And believe it or not, moles do have their benefits. The moles burrowing in a lawn help to loosen and aerate the soil, therefore increasing the soil's ability to retain moisture. In heavy rains the mole tunnels also drain away the excess water.

Moles are difficult to evict from a lawn. Some people claim mothballs placed in the mole burrows encourage the miners to move elsewhere. I have never tried it because I kind of like the down-to-earth animals.

FARM LIST

Twenty-five years ago we started keeping annual lists of birds seen on our 120-acre farm. Then in 1976, the bicentennial year, we compiled those lists into a farm life list. It is still the only life list of birds I keep. We used the order of appearance in the field guides, and the pied-billed grebe was number one. This little ducklike diver (it has the unique ability to swim along and sink out of sight at the same time, submerging like a submarine) was seen a few times over the years on our farm pond. The last bird on the list, number 135, was the snow bunting.

Of those 135 species, only one wasn't seen by at least one member of our family, and that was the ruffed grouse. The last grouse seen in this neighborhood for almost fifty years was shot by a hunter in our grapevine-filled woods in the early 1940s. It was a bird-in-hand deal, so its identification wasn't questioned and the grouse made the list as a bird seen on the farm.

Over the ten years that followed 1976, twenty-nine more species were added, from the whistling (tundra) swan to the bald eagle. Some of interest were the common goldeneye, a diving duck, and the handsome hooded merganser, both on the pond. Two white-winged scoters, sea ducks, circled the pond in 1978 but didn't stop; so did a small flock of black terns. In April 1984, a sandhill crane flew over the farm. I was working in the fields when the crane's weird call attracted my attention and I saw it, long neck outstretched, overhead. Number 163.

The next ten years averaged only one new bird per year. One was a duck, the gadwall. Three were warblers, the Kentucky, prairie, and hooded. And I saw the first woodcock on the farm in November 1987. I was repairing the line-fence through the woods when a brown bird flushed from almost underfoot. The bird was plump with an oversized bill attached to a huge head. Its flight down the fence line was erratic but swift, and I was delighted to have the woodcock for a new neighbor. A western meadowlark traveled east in 1993. Its lovely flutelike song reached our ears as he sang from a perch in a neighboring field.

This past week, for the first time in many years, I added two new birds to the list. On the 24th of March I spotted a common loon cleaving the farm from south to north high overhead. Propelled by a strong tailwind, the big bird wasn't wasting time on its long journey back to its breeding grounds—or waters—in the north country.

Loons are designed for life on the water. With their legs set far to the back of their bodies, loons are able to dive great depths for fish. On land, however, they are awkward. Friends of ours once found a loon near Fredericksburg that had mistaken a rain-slickened road for a river and landed. Once on the road, the loon was unable to take off, since it requires a "run" across the surface of the water to become airborne. The helpless loon needed to be tossed into the air before it could continue its journey.

The wildly hilarious laughter of the loon is a common summertime sound on the lakes of Canada and Minnesota—a call of the wilderness that adds extra meaning to the phrases "loony" and "crazy as a loon" (although both expressions could have derived from the word *loon*, they actually come from the word *lunatic*).

7

In comparison to the hustling loon, the herring gull I saw on the 27th was merely loitering. The large white gull with its black-tipped wings would catch an updraft, circle high, and then drop back down to check things out closer to earth. Slowly it wound its way north toward Lake Erie. The gull is now number 175, the last entry on the list.

In this cold weather, with the passerine bird migration pretty well on hold, skywatching still has its rewards. The day I saw the gull was sunny, with the wind out of the east. I was clearing out brush along a fence line and tidying up behind the county roadside brush-whacker—a work that leaves a residue about as elegant as a city dump. Before roadside fields can be plowed, the chewed-off branches and old steel fence posts that were flung fifty feet into the field by the whacker have to be picked up. I kept a pair of binoculars on the wagon, and if a speck in the sky showed promise, I grabbed the glasses and looked. Since birds have that marvelous ability to fly, one never knows what to expect. Most specks were local red-tailed hawks enjoying the ideal soaring weather. One, though, turned out to be a Boeing.

THE LION'S TOOTH

In the next week or two the dandelions will be in full bloom. Few things can transcend the beauty of grazing animals in lush pastureland strewn with the rich-toned yellow of dandelion blossoms—if, that is, the beholder can look at the dandelion as a thing of beauty instead of as a weed. Which, I must admit, is sometimes difficult to do.

The dandelion, a relative of lettuce, was called *dent de lion* by the French because the jagged edges of the leaves reminded them of the teeth of a lion.

The problem with the "lion's tooth" is that it grows where it's not wanted. A perennial, it does especially well in lawns and hay fields, where it sends its long taproot down to moisture and nutrients with the intentions of staying for a long time. In drought years, when the shallow-rooted grasses in lawns turn brown from lack of water, the dandelion stays nice and green, like sprigs of parsley garnishing a platter of cheeses.

Should the angry lawn owner seek revenge by cutting off the dandelion plant, the remaining portion of taproot will send up two to four new plants the next spring—sometimes in a neat little circle.

Probably out of frustration with the failure of manual control, many people go after dandelions with weed killers. Unfortunately, dandelion-killing chemicals also kill other broadleaf plants such as the white clovers, which are beneficial in lawns as builders of soil fertility. In the 1980s more of the herbicide 2,4-D was used on suburban lawns, mainly to control dandelions, than on agricultural land.

We quit warring with the dandelion years ago. Well, not entirely: we eat it, though only in early April when the plants are still young and tender, and before they set flower heads and become bitter. Prepared as a sweet-and-sour gravy, the dandelion is delicious over potatoes, rice, or pasta. The gravy is made with bacon, flour, milk, a little sugar, salt to taste, cider vinegar, and at least four or five sliced hard-boiled eggs. Just before serving, the washed, crisp dandelion greens are added. Locally, dandelion gravy is considered such a delicacy that at least one restaurant, Boyd and Wurthman's in Berlin, had it on their menu this week.

Part of the affection for dandelion greens is that it is the first salad of the spring; to me it even tastes like spring. Plus the greens have more vitamins A and C than lettuce and more iron than spinach.

I love it when parts of our lawn and fields become seas of yellow flowers—evidence of man's failure to control nature. It's easier to imitate nature than to fight it. When the dandelions go to seed is when they lose their beauty. It is close to the epitome of ugliness to see otherwise well-manicured lawns sprout a new crop of protruding seed heads only hours after being mowed. Almost as ugly as plastic flamingos.

But who doesn't remember, as a child, holding a fully ripe seedhead of dandelion on a calm May day and then blowing it and watching the downy seeds drift to earth. You blew three times, and the number of seeds left told how many children you would have. Another version had it that the number of seeds left told the time of day.

Even though millions of dollars are being spent to control the dandelion, its seeds are still listed in several seed catalogs. While some are eradicating, others are sowing.

NIGHTCRAWLERS

After what seemed like an incredibly long time, it rained. A good rain, over an inch. Over three million gallons on our 120 acres. I feel like celebrating. So did the nightcrawlers, because this morning our lawn was literally covered with them, like scattered spaghetti. The crawlers had come to the surface to fully experience the blessed rain, and to feed and to mate.

I wasn't aware until recently that the nightcrawler is not a native to this continent, or so it's thought. Nobody really seems to know for sure.

It has been suggested that the nightcrawler, or its lemon-shaped cocoons, hitched a ride across the Atlantic in the soil of potted plants brought by the early European settlers. From there it crawled west and became a successful and useful resident in the fertile soils of the New World. (As to its usefulness, just ask any Lake Erie walleye fisherman.)

When the nightcrawler leaves its burrow to feed, it keeps its foot in the doorway for a quick retreat in case of danger. Even though the nightcrawler has no ears or eyes, it is very sensitive to vibrations and light. When I walked through our lawn, the slight sound of my footfall sent most of the crawlers within three or four feet back into their burrows. Daybreak chased the rest of them home.

All, that is, except for the careless pairs still locked in a gluey embrace. To engage in such activity in a yard full of robins is definitely not safe. For a while I thought the robins might need help getting airborne.

As all robins must know, and any person who has attempted

it knows, pulling a nightcrawler from its burrow can be tough. The reason is that its skin has retractable bristles, or setae, which grip the walls of the burrow when the worm is threatened. Should the nightcrawler snap in two, only the part that contains the middle, or central nerve network, will grow a new end.

Nevertheless, pulling nightcrawlers from their burrows has become big business, especially in parts of southern Ontario, where millions are harvested for the U.S. bait market. A good picker may gather eight to ten thousand worms on a good night. Many of those crawlers end up in bait shops along the south shore of Lake Erie, where they are sold to fishermen for two dollars a dozen.

Nightcrawlers should not be looked on only as fish bait, but also as creatures vital to the life in the soil. It has been estimated that an acre may contain as many as fifty thousand earthworms, which in a year bring fifteen to twenty tons of soil to the surface in their castings, or excrement. This greatly enriches the soil's fertility. Our quality of life depends a lot on the lowly worm. They help us garden and farm.

They also help in aerating and draining the soil with their burrows. During my early school years there was always a wet spot (not quite a wetland) behind shortstop on our softball field. One morning the teacher came to school with a gallon can partly filled with nightcrawlers. These were spread behind short, and in a few days the seep disappeared. No more sliding in mud.

In the eighteenth century the British clergyman Gilbert White wrote in *The Natural History of Selborne:* "The earth without worms would soon become cold, hard-bound, and sterile." And, I could add, wet behind short.

GRAY TREEFROG

Spring has promises to keep, and must leave——to be replaced with the heat and sounds of summer. As the season progresses, the natural sounds that accompany it change along with it. While the daylight hours are filled with bird song, the evenings and nights still belong to the frogs. (With competition from a lone mockingbird that has been singing all night. Perhaps the heat has gotten to him.) Although lately the songs of the peepers and toads have faded, a new sound has seized the evenings: the call of the gray treefrog. To me, this is a sound of June and somnolent early-summer nights.

Ever since the first pipings of the spring peepers back in early April, there has been a constant chorus, interrupted now and then by cold weather, of evening sounds. While the chirping peepers and singing toads needed a whole throng to garner one's attention, on these warm and humid nights the loud trilling call of a single treefrog is just as ear-catching.

The song of the treefrog is a short musical trill, somewhat resembling the call of the red-bellied woodpecker. It is much louder and more frantic and of shorter duration than the lingering and softer tremulous call of the American toad.

The other night, lying in bed, I listened to five or six calling treefrogs. Each had a slightly different pitch to his love song (only the males sing). So I got a flashlight and my watch, concentrated on the one closest to the house, and timed it. The trilling burst of song lasted one second; there was a pause of three seconds while he caught his breath, and the song was repeated. The result was fifteen calls a minute that went on without interruption for three or four hours. And a friend of mine claims he couldn't do without his classical music!

Interestingly, treefrogs cease their calling soon after midnight. I can only guess at what happens between then and the dawn. Maybe they leave their trilling perches in the maple trees and go for a moonlight swim in the pond. Only rarely is a treefrog still calling when I bring the cows past the pond in the coolness of early morning.

The gray treefrog has the unique ability to change its color to match its habitat. Hence its scientific name, *Hyla versicolor.* The one we found the other evening clinging to the siding of the house was greenish gray etched with irregular black lines across its back. The inside of its thighs were vivid orange—a bright contrast to its gray back and white underside. Later on in the summer, when the treefrog spends most of its time foraging in the trees, its color may be light green to match the leaves.

Because their toe ends have little suction cups, treefrogs are amazingly agile and are able to cling to almost any surface. The one on our house had no problem hanging on to the siding or leaping to the chimney and clinging to the bricks. I've had treefrogs cling to my shirt, their tiny throats pulsating in fright or excitement. We carried the one on the house to the maple in the front yard and watched as it effortlessly hopped up the tree. It never called during the night, so it likely was a female searching for the songsters.

Worldwide, frogs have fallen on hard times. Scientists aren't exactly sure why, but they do agree that there is a problem: frogs are vanishing. Possible reasons are the continuing pollution of wetlands and the depletion of the ozone layer in the stratosphere, which allows more ultraviolet radiation to reach the earth, affecting the fertility of newly laid frog eggs.

Locally I've seen a decline in the numbers of spring peepers—a decline that began when the local population of Canada geese started increasing. A peeper to a hungry goose is what a bite-sized Snickers is to a human. The gray treefrogs seem to be increasing in number, which is good, because they are the only ones with a song strong enough to carry spring into summer.

BIRDS' NESTS

Every morning when I walk to the barn I pass by the Colorado blue spruce where a mourning dove has a nest. The nest is only about a foot above eye level, so I try to be careful not to startle the dove, since her nest, if it can be called a nest, offers little protection for the two white eggs. Should the dove be spooked by the lantern light, the eggs would likely fall to the ground and break.

While the mourning dove is not a master nest builder, many other birds around our farm are. As I write this, a female cardinal is sitting on her superior nest less than three feet away in a spirea bush. Even though she can see me inside the window, she shows no fear. Oftentimes she sits with her eyes closed and, on cool days, with her reddish bill tucked beneath her wing. From all appearances it seems like a pretty easy job. Actually, though, the twelve days of incubation is about the only time the female cardinal gets any rest during the nesting season.

It was interesting for us to watch the buff-brown female cardinal build her nest. She got no help from her red-feathered mate. Once she was satisfied that the foundation twigs were in their proper place, the nest progressed steadily as she kept adding twigs until the rough platform of the nest had taken shape. Then began the most tedious part of making the nest. First using finer twigs, and then rootlets and grasses, she began shaping the nest cup. Every so often she would hop in, squat down, and then, while kicking her feet, turn around and around in the nest. Once in a while she would pause and, with her bill, tuck at and rearrange some of the twigs and grasses until the nest had the right feel. The final touch was a lining of horse hair. From start to finish it took her almost three days.

Several more days went by before the first grayish blotched-with-brown egg appeared in the nest. Two more eggs were laid on successive days, and then the female cardinal began incubating—and resting. Not always, though. The other day it stormed and rained two inches and the fragile-looking nest and its occupants had a wild ride. While the winds whipped the bushes and the hard rains beat down, the cardinal stayed in the nest and rode out the storm. To her, the most important thing in the world was her eggs—the future of her kind.

While birds' nests vary in shape and form almost as much as the birds themselves, they do fall roughly into three categories. The first, and most primitive, type is the scrape nest, where a shallow cup is hollowed out of the ground or in leaves. The killdeer nest is a good example. These common plovers make a slight depression, often in tilled fields; the only nesting material is a collection of small pebbles and maybe a few shreds of old corn stalks. The female then lays her four (only rarely three or five) large pointed-at-one-end eggs, which closely resemble the gravel-lined nest. Even the incubating killdeer is hard to see with its earth-colored back and white breast striped with black. Perfect camouflage.

The second type is the platform nest used by hawks, herons, and some marsh-nesting birds like the common moorhen. A pair of green herons build a flimsy platform nest in a wild apple tree in our woods. The nest is so crude that the pale green eggs can be seen through the sticks that form its structure. In spite of the poorly made nest, almost every summer we see young herons trying their luck at fishing in the pond.

By far the most artistic and commonest type is the cup nest

built by the songbird family. But even cup nests vary greatly, some consisting solely of hundreds of mud pellets stuck together by cliff swallows, or sticks glued together with saliva and stuck to the inside of chimneys by chimney swifts. These are called adherent cup nests.

Probably the most intricate cup nests are the pendulous nests built by flycatchers, vireos, and orioles. Made out of plant fibers, yarn, twine, grapevine bark, and lined with long hairs from the tails of horses and cows, the hanging basket nest of the Baltimore oriole is a common dooryard sight. Usually suspended from a drooping branch on the outer edge of large trees, the tough-woven nest will weather all but the severest summer storms.

Almost one-fourth of the songbirds in North America are cavity nesters or build covered nests. Some of these, like bluebirds and tree swallows, build cup nests inside manmade boxes or in natural cavities. Bluebirds line their nest with grasses, while tree swallows use feathers. Another cavity nester, the tufted titmouse, lines its nest with moss, hair, and fur.

Last spring we watched a titmouse gather fur for its nest. It was a warm day in May and we were looking for warblers when we spotted a small bird high in a willow tree. The bird—it turned out to be a titmouse—was plucking fur from a raccoon that was attempting to sleep in a crotch of the tree! Alighting on the animal's rump, the titmouse would grab a billful of fur, brace its feet, and jerk. Evidently not all the fur was old and being shed by the coon because occasionally it would raise its head, snarl, and then snap at the titmouse, which hurriedly darted out of reach. As soon as the coon dozed off, the titmouse went back to work.

While most birds build new nests for every brood, there are a few exceptions to this rule, notably the barn and cliff swallows. These birds may add some new nest lining, but usually as soon as the first brood has fledged, a second clutch of eggs is laid. Some birds even use the nests of other species. Great horned owls take over a hawks' or crows' nests for their own. And quite often a mourning dove will use an old robin's nest to raise her family—a nest that is a lot sturdier and more secure than their own.

Last summer I even heard of a bird moving its nest to a safer place for a second nesting attempt. Friends of ours had a pair of ruby-throated hummingbirds build their tiny, delicate nest close to their house. Soon after the female began incubating, the two pea-sized eggs disappeared. Alvin blamed a pair of house wrens that had a nest nearby. In any case, the female hummingbird dismantled the old nest and moved it bit by bit to a new location on the other side of the summer house, away from the feisty wrens. Once the nest was finished, complete with lichens on its sides, she laid two more eggs and successfully raised the young. I had never before heard of such behavior in hummingbirds, or any other birds for that matter.

Our friendly cardinal's eggs must be close to hatching because she almost never leaves the nest to feed. This morning she even whistled her cardinal song while sitting on the nest. Then the male brought some food and fed her. Afterward she called out her rain song, "Wet! Wet! Wet!" It figures—we mowed hay yesterday.

FLIES

Last night it rained. A soft gentle rain, so unlike the many raging storms of this summer. This rain came like Carl Sandburg's fog—"on little cat feet." Already I can sense, with the soft rain, a slowing of the season, that winding down as summer begins its leisurely drift toward autumn.

The signs of a waning season are everywhere: starlings and blackbirds are congregating, and every evening great flocks fly in a northwesterly direction to roost for the night; the purple martins and bobolinks are departing, and the bluebird house at the end of the hay field has been empty since the brood of tree swallows left it two weeks ago.

Now, a month since the summer solstice, the sun is edging southward and the daylight hours are noticeably shorter. In the bottomlands, joe-pye and ironweed are showing some color, promising seas of lavender and deep purple throughout late summer. In the world of the insects, however, the peak is yet to come. Soon the nightly chorus of the treefrogs will be replaced by the scratching notes of the katydids. And the daytime melodies will be rasped by cicadas and buzzed by flies.

Flies—houseflies, stable flies, blowflies, horseflies, face flies, horn flies—are everywhere. The other day a piglet got caught between the fence and its mother, and several days went by in the busyness of the harvest before I got around to giving it a decent burial. By then the green blowflies had done their grisly work and the pig was in the process of being devoured by their maggots. Thousands of them. Along with the turkey vulture, the blowfly is nature's way of keeping the countryside neat and tidy.

Many flies, like the horse and horn, are biting flies and suck blood from their animal hosts. Face flies and houseflies, on the other hand, are sucking flies. The face flies feed on the secretions around the eyes and nostrils of large animals and can spread bacterial diseases like pinkeye. In years of heavy infestations, usually following mild winters, face flies are extremely annoying to horses and cattle. Houseflies, as we all know, prefer jelly and going along on picnics, where potato salad and pies are their favorites. Spilled Pepsi is fine too.

When a housefly hits the jackpot at a picnic, its probiscis telescopes downward and the fleshy lobes at the end spread out. Then the fly begins pumping the sweet liquid, be it baked beans or the juice of grilled burgers, up through the tube to its stomach and, unless shooed or swatted, feeds until it is satiated.

A female housefly will lay her 75 to 120 eggs in manure or garbage. The eggs hatch within twenty-four hours and ten days later will be adult flies. While the male housefly lives only two weeks, the female can survive for a month if there is food available.

There have been several campaigns to rid the nation of the housefly once and for all. The first, early in this century, was basically a swatting campaign. After an attempt was made to eliminate fly breeding sites, the flies that were left over were swatted. In Washington, D.C., a group of children killed 350,000 flies and won a twenty-five-dollar first prize. The effort failed to eradicate the housefly.

The next great hope arose when DDT was developed during World War II. The insecticide was declared a "veritable godsend" by public health officials seeking to control the pesky flies, and DDT worked fantastically. For a while. Then the lowly housefly began to develop resistance to DDT, and also, people began to notice that songbirds were disappearing in heavily sprayed areas. The "godsend" began to unravel.

Ever since, flies have continued to build resistance to new insecticides within a few years after they're introduced. The fly sprays that worked superbly on cattle two decades ago are virtually worthless today. One fly spray sold by the local feed store is called Ce-Em-Die, which, the local farmers say, is a misnomer: it should be Ce-Em-Fly.

Maybe St. Augustine's idea that God created flies to punish human arrogance is right and they will always be here to pester us. But flies do serve a useful purpose in the intricate scheme of nature. After all, if I hadn't buried the pig, the flies would have done the job for me.

LIFE ON THE MAPLE

Soon after my parents started farming here in 1938 they planted a silver maple on the south side of the house. On the east side of the house is a hand-dug well that furnishes us with fresh drinking water. The 165-year-old well is only eighteen feet deep and is laid up with round fieldstones, most of them Canadian Shield granite. The well, in a sense, is a developed spring, and the silver maple, like a tree growing by a river, flourishes with its feet in the good spring water.

The other day our daughter Emily and I measured the fifty-five-year-old tree: at chest height it is seventeen feet and three inches in circumference, with a crown at least seventy feet across.

Silver maples are native to river bottoms and floodplains, where they should stay. People plant silver maples because of their rapid growth. Nobody wants to wait on the slower-growing sugar maple, a more pleasing tree. The sugar maple is a hardwood—close-grained, rich in color, and excellent for furniture and hardwood flooring. The wood is as pretty as the tree's autumn hues.

The sugar maple is my violin-playing friend's favorite tree because its hard wood is used for the backs of violins. (The tops are spruce.) The sixteenth- and seventeenth-century Amanti family violins have maple backs, as do the ones of their famous apprentice, Antonio Stradivari. Maple, for some reason, produces the perfect sweetness of tone.

Even though I would prefer a sugar maple, I love the massive silver maple in our yard and wouldn't give it up for anything—even in spite of its disadvantages. Since it is a fast-growing tree, its wood is soft and brittle. During ice storms huge limbs often break under the tons of ice and crash to the roof of the house. Nail-biting conditions.

Unlike the small, winged seeds of the sugar maple, which ripen in late summer, the much larger and more numerous silver maple seeds ripen in late spring. Every year I hope for a freeze in late March that will kill most of the young seeds forming on the early-blooming tree. My hopes are usually fulfilled, and the tree bears seeds only one year out of four. But the year it does bear there are tens of thousands of them, which ripen in early June.

Ripening just in time for one of the season's first storms, a swarm of winged seeds rides the crest of the wind eastward to colonize gardens and fields and fill all eaves troughs, including barns'. Actually, it is a thrilling sight to watch the seeds helicopter to new territory. A month later the downspouts begin sprouting green maple trees from the joints and I clean hundreds of seedlings from the gutters.

Those are the flaws of the silver maple. Now, its good points. The tree provides us much pleasure, besides its refreshing shade. Baltimore and orchard orioles, warbling vireos, robins, mourning doves, mallard ducks, and a pair of starlings nest in the tree. Most provide lovely songs into midsummer.

This past summer two fox squirrels moved into our yard to feed on unsprouted maple seeds, and claimed the maple tree for their home. (Unlike homes in the city, squirrels are rare in most rural yards—too many farm dogs around.) Since the maple tree has no hollowed-out dens, save for the woodpecker burrow the starlings usurped, the squirrels built a leaf nest high in one of the forks. The squirrels also gathered pieces of baler twine and used it in their nest-building, apparently to tie things down in case of fierce storms.

Right now the annual cicadas are leaving the ground around the maple tree; they climb partway up the trunk, where they then split their last nymphal skin and emerge as adults. While the periodical cicadas have life cycles of thirteen or seventeen years, a generation of annual cicadas (so called because a brood emerges every summer), sometimes called locusts, leaves the ground every year after feeding as nymphs for three to five years on the sweet juice of the maple's roots.

The other morning we found a cicada on the maple's bark that was just ready to emerge from its nymphal stage. We took it into the house to watch while we ate breakfast. After it had ruptured the skin lengthwise down its back, it took the cicada half an hour to crawl out and be free of its flightless shell. What surprised me was the absence of wings. It had two stubs, which looked like the plucked wings of an inch-and-a-half-long chicken. The stubs showed no hint of the long membranous wings adult cicadas have.

For an hour the cicada didn't move except occasionally to sort of jerk. Then tiny wings began to sprout from the stubs, which seemed to act as a signal for the cicada to go through several convulsions, like a hunk flexing his muscles, and within a few seconds the long gauzy wings unfolded. The soft wings rippled gently in the slight breeze. (By now we had moved the cicada back to the tree.)

All forenoon the cicada remained almost motionless as it dried and darkened, a process entomologists call tanning. By noon its wings had turned from light green to a dark transparent green. Its body also turned a deeper shade of green. Five hours after emerging from its flightless larval shell, the cicada climbed farther up into the maple and began the final stage of its life.

If the cicada is a male, he will soon begin singing his loud song, which rises to a shrill rasp and ends in a descending buzz. Unlike many of August's singing insects, which fiddle in the grateful coolness of the night, cicadas sing during the heat of the day. Their song goes with harvest time. In New England the cicada is called the Dogday Harvestfly.

THE OTHER GARDEN

We have two permanent gardens. The big one could be called our serious garden. It is large, between the house and the orchard, and it is here that we grow the bulk of the tomatoes and vegetables that will end up in hundreds of mason jars in the cellar and see our family through the coming winter.

So naturally, when the seed catalogs and the *Seed Savers Yearbook* arrive in January, it is on the big garden that we focus. (Usually we plant our sweet corn and potatoes somewhere in the crop fields to confuse the insects. Last year our potato patch was so well hidden that only a few Colorado potato beetles managed to find it.)

The other garden is smaller and more unfettered. But it is just as important, I think, as the main garden—and thereon hangs this tale.

Since the garden is virtually on our doorstep, its food function is mainly as a provider of fresh salad makings—lettuces, broccoli, cauliflower, radishes, onions, a few cucumber plants, and several Siberian tomatoes—that end up on the dinner table only minutes after leaving the garden. However, only about half of the garden space is for our culinary benefit. The rest tends toward the wild—plantings for birds and butterflies and beauty, annuals and perennials.

Most of the perennials are native to this part of the country: the wild rose, butterfly weed, black-eyed Susan, hepatica, bergamot, purple violet, and New England aster. And most have a story that explains their appearance in our garden.

Friends from the Shenandoah Valley brought us the hepatica. A local friend gave us the wild rose.

I dug up the black-eyed Susan from a neighbor's hay field that was to be plowed. We had noticed the flowers in bloom throughout the late summer in a field that was too sparse to cut for hay. The following January, during a thaw and after getting permission from the farmer, I went to the field and brought the clump of Susans home in a five-gallon bucket and planted it next to the coreopsis.

To my chagrin I read soon afterward that the black-eyed Susan is a biennial, which means that after blooming and forming seeds in its second summer, it dies. So I had transplanted a dead plant. Oh well, I thought, at least we tried to save the plant from the plow. Even in its deadness, the dried brown eyes were pretty, so we left it undisturbed through the spring. Sometime in early June, the clump began sprouting promising-looking leaves, and in July the first of thirty-eight flowers opened. What really amazed us was that the yellow-petaled flowers stayed nice until frost put them down.

Our striking deep-blue New England asters, to me the prettiest of the aster clan, we found growing abundantly on the farm of friends in the western part of the state. They generously gave us several for our garden.

An annual flower that was given to us by our neighbors in the threshing ring and now sprouts from seeds in the garden is the electric light. Another local name for the lavender-and-white flower is fire light. Bees love its nectar, which they gather only in the early morning and late evening. Hummingbirds also visit the flowers.

Other of our annuals are mixed zinnias, impatiens, petunias, and Mexican sunflowers. (These come from Burpee.) Swallowtail butterflies especially are attracted to the zinnias.

A few perennials from Burpee that add beauty and are loved by the butterflies and bees are the purple coneflowers and shasta daisies.

Other birds besides the nectar-sipping hummingbirds frequent the garden. In fact, about thirty pairs live in the garden. On a pole near the garden's center is a forty-compartment purple martin house. Not only do the graceful birds eat many pesky flying insects, they also make music for us all the day. My wife insists that the martins seem the happiest when she is working underneath their home. Chipping sparrows nesting in the nearby evergreen and apple trees do a lot of their food gathering in the garden. Cabbage loopers are to young chipping sparrows what pizzas are to teenaged humans.

Maybe the main reason I love this part-tame, part-wild garden so much is that it is located between the house and the barn. When I go to or leave the house, I often linger for several minutes there. Perhaps I'll eat a radish or a tender green onion, but more often I just pause to watch the life of the garden. What is going on may determine my day's work. If it's morning and there is hay to be made, I watch the wild things: if the bees and birds are exceptionally active and the maple leaves show their undersides in the slight breeze, I'll figure rain may be coming and probably change our plans from hay mowing to corn cultivating (or maybe fishing).

I also like to sit on the other side of the garden, on the porch of an 1800s log cabin we restored. It is here that I often close out the summer days—sometimes by reading, but more often just by sitting and reflecting (maybe meditating would be a better word) on the day's farm work, surrounded by the ambience of times past, the beauty of the present, and the promise of the future.

I watch the children play a game of pitch-and-catch across

from the garden. As the darkness gathers, the purple martins return to their home in the garden. From the sound of their pleasant voices, I can tell they had a good day. Then there is the hum of swift wings as a sphinx moth arrives and sips nectar from a variety of flowers. The children's ball game is called off because of lack of light, even though the fireflies do their utmost to illuminate the outfield and the gray treefrogs trill for more play. The children, after getting refreshing drinks of water at the pump, say they, too, had a good day.

We all did.

THE JOY OF BUTTERFLIES

Now that the midpoint of summer has arrived along with the heat of August, the birds' nesting season is winding down. In fact, many of the neotropical birds that migrate north to this region to nest have already left, such as the pair of Baltimore orioles that entertained us all spring and early summer with song and color. They raised their family in a pendulum-like nest high on the south side of the maple tree and have been gone since mid-July. But just as colorful as the orioles are the numerous butterflies that can be seen right now and throughout August.

In grade school I had the good fortune of having a naturalist-teacher who knew the joy of butterflies. When school began in early September we would spend the first two weeks racing across fields with nets in the pursuit of swallowtails and fritillaries and viceroys and a dozen other kinds. Of course, in the perfect weather of late summer, softball was factored in, and if any time was left over we worked on our lessons in the classroom. But our minds were outdoors.

We would hide the little *Golden Guide to Butterflies and Moths* behind the geography textbook and dream of rare butterflies. Dancing through our minds were giant and zebra swallowtails, regal and varied fritillaries, and the Diana. The fritillaries we found a few times, but it wasn't until many years later that I saw my first giant swallowtail, and then some more years before coming across the zebra swallowtail. I still haven't met Diana.

Even though the range maps show the giant and zebra

swallowtails this far north, the host plants for their caterpillars are southern trees. The larvae of the giant swallowtail feed on citrus trees, and those of the zebra on pawpaw trees. Naturally, we're out of the range of the citrus, and we're right on the northern fringe of the pawpaw. The pawpaw is common in southern Ohio—and so is the zebra swallowtail.

Every year we plant flowers attractive to butterflies. For a few years we had a row of Mexican sunflowers in the garden. One day, during my noon siesta time, the children came running and said there was a new, and huge, butterfly on the sunflowers. When I reached the garden they were ready to capture the visitor in their combination minnow-butterfly-snake net. To my amazement, the butterfly was a giant swallowtail, and it deftly avoided capture. Having waited thirty years to see one, I grabbed the net and caught the butterfly for a better look. After a few minutes of gently holding and admiring the rare beauty, we released it and watched it lift into the warm summer sky.

The only zebra swallowtail I have seen on our farm was flying—actually, bee-lining would be a better description—across the hay field assisted by a strong tail wind. No hands-on inspection of it!

Biologists call butterflies an indicator species: they reveal a lot about the health of an ecosystem. If their numbers are down, there is a problem somewhere. I'm surprised that any giant swallowtails survive with citrus as host plants for their caterpillars, since we consumers of oranges and grapefruits demand a blemish-free fruit. Insecticides used in orchards kill the good along with the ugly.

The happy news is that many species of butterflies are doing well, at least around here. Right in front of me, in our salad and butterfly garden, I see a Milbert's tortoise shell on the butterfly bush, a tiger swallowtail on the zinnias, several great spangled fritillaries on the coneflowers, and cabbage butterflies on—what else?—the cabbage. (Interestingly, there's also a hummingbird moth, which looks like a tiny tailless hummingbird as it zips from flower to flower. It is one of the few moths that feeds in the daytime.)

Often overlooked are the small butterflies, those smaller than two inches across, which include the blues, satyrs, skippers, hairstreaks, checkerspots, coppers, and elfins—a fascinating realm where bifocals become necessary.

SPIDERS

A voice from out of the dust:

"Do you know what I like about sweeping down cobwebs?"

"No."

"Nothing!"

That's close to my sentiments, too. But then I see how nice and clean the milking stable looks where it has been swept and I know the milk inspector will be happy. Reward enough.

I have explained the value of spiders in controlling stable flies, which the inspector also abhors, but she is unimpressed. Neither does the inspector see merit in having spiders around in case of an injury to man or beast so that cobwebs might be used to stem the flow of blood. So we sweep down webs.

Overnight the webs reappear. It takes time, however, for the silken nets to accumulate dust and become annoying, giving us a six-month break before Martha spies them again.

Spiders rank right up there with snakes and bats as the most hated creatures in nature. I could never understand why: spiders have always fascinated me. Even the ones in the barn. When we sweep their webs, we never hurt the spiders because they know what's coming and hide in the corners.

I must admit, I don't love them so much that I want to share a bath with those big hairy wolf spiders that at times slip into the tub and can't climb up the smooth sides. For them, it's a hot-water flush down the drain.

Unlike our barn spiders and many others, the wolf spider does not use a web to capture insects. Instead it lies in wait and pounces on its prey, such as flies or earwigs, when they come within reach.

It is the web-spinning spider that is the real artist. A few weeks ago on one of those crisp upper-forties mornings, I was walking down the road when suddenly I noticed the spider webs: the orb-weavers had been busy. The delicate new webs, up to a foot across, were everywhere—hanging from grasses, small trees, and wire fences. All were dew covered and sagging a bit, which in the early morning sunlight added extra beauty.

Many of the orb-weavers spin a new web each day, usually over the course of about an hour in the early evening, after having eaten the remains of the day-old web. They're the original recyclers.

The black-and-yellow argiope, what some call the garden spider, so common around homes, in shrubbery and gardens, and along roadsides, is an orb-weaver. The female of this beneficial and nonpoisonous species of spiders is often over an inch long, with an abdomen as round as a small marble. She builds a large and beautiful web strong enough to hold small grasshoppers. Between the grasshopper's kicks, she wraps it in silk. When the struggles cease, she dines.

The morning of all the webs I closely examined one. It was larger than the others, nearly twenty inches in diameter. It was unique in that around the outside the web was of normal thickness, while the center had silk so fine that no dew showed on the almost invisible threads. How clever. Its purpose was obvious: any insect flying toward the web would try to escape through the "open" center and get trapped.

Spider silk stretches like rubber, yet for its thickness it's stronger than steel—as those grasshoppers in the argiope's web have found out. On sunny windy days, young spiders often climb on twigs or fence posts and release a thread of silk into the wind until there is enough pull to take them sailing into new territory. Young spiders have shown up on ships far out at sea.

Spiders are not true insects in that they have eight legs instead of six, and instead of having three sections like insects, spiders come in two parts. The head and the chest are one piece called the cephalothorax (all eight legs are attached to this section); the other part is the abdomen. Spiders can see quite well, since most species also have eight eyes—one eye for each leg.

Like Homo sapiens, spiders come in all shapes and forms: thin, fat; short-legged, long-legged; docile, mean; interesting, dull—three thousand species in North America alone. As Annie Dillard wrote, "I allow them to run the place."

THE CROW

When the ground is frozen and the frigid winds known as Alberta Clippers whip across the snowbound fields, our manure spreader is the bringer of good things for the small band of crows that choose to endure the northern winter on our farm. The crows know quite well that the farm is a place not only of life but also of death. Be it piglets flattened by a careless mother, a barn cat caught beneath a Percheron's heavy hoof, or the waste parts from a butchered cow—eventually the manure spreader will transport death to the fields. In crowdom this machine must rate as one of the cleverest devices ever designed by humans.

Last week when we cleaned out the barn, the first load of manure carried along a few of the accumulated casualties. In the nearby woods the crows were waiting. When I came with the second load, they were already feeding on the deposited carcasses. Normally cautious birds, these crows allowed me to approach fairly close before they strode away and then reluctantly took wing, flinging a few annoyed "caw! caw's!" back at me. Flying only a short distance, they landed and waited for me to leave.

The heavy hand of winter forces the crows to become carrion eaters in order to survive. When farmers do not furnish their food, the crows resort to road kills. Cottontail rabbits, which are active all winter, are the crows' main road fare. An opossum venturing across the road during a winter thaw and getting hit by a car will do just fine as well. How crows manage to feed on road kills without getting hit themselves is a wonder. Often waiting until the last second before opening their wings, the crows deftly avoid the speeding traffic. I have seen road-killed creatures ranging from a white-tailed deer to a screech owl—even a turkey vulture—but never a crow. Crows are simply too clever to get smashed.

Scientists believe that the family Corvidae, to which the crow belongs, has the highest level of bird intelligence, since the brain in comparison to body size is the largest among all birds. Others in the loudmouthed but flashy clan are the ravens, jays, nutcrackers, and magpies—and in the Old World, rooks and jackdaws. One does not have to observe crows for very long to become a believer in their smartness.

I once had a pet crow—pilfered from a nest of four young. I was fourteen when the less-than-two-weeks-old crow came to our household in early May. On a diet of hard-boiled eggs, bread soaked in milk, and cheese, "Crow" grew remarkably fast and became as tame as a kitten. Although male and female crows look alike, I always took Crow to be a male, mostly because of its show-off ways.

When Crow was fully feathered and learned to fly, his antics began in earnest. Loving small objects—especially shiny things—Crow gathered pieces of colored glass, nails, and clothespins, and even cleaned out the open toolbox on the Oliver hay mower of nuts and bolts. He hid his treasures in odd places around the buildings.

Crow also had quite a vocabulary. Not human sounds, but bird language. In the morning he would "sing" for us—a soft, guttural, almost cooing sound. During the day Crow would often mimic the calls of other birds. He never cawed. Was that something that had to be leaned from other crows?

When we worked in the fields, Crow went along. He often rode on the backs of the horses, a habit that worried my uncle, who owned a spooky mule named Jim. One day while I was helping my uncle bale hay, he warned: "If that crow lands on Jim's back, there is no man in this whole world who will be able to hold that mule!" Fortunately Crow didn't sit on the mule, although I think he was tempted.

If someone in a car stopped by, one of Crow's favorite thrills was to perch on the hood of the car, clamp one black foot over the hood ornament, and go along for a feather-ruffling ride. Facing into the wind, Crow would hang on until the speed became too great; then he would spread his wings and whoosh over the top of the car. On arriving back at the house he would preen his mussed feathers, obviously pleased with his performance.

Toward the end of summer Crow became wiser—at least in his own eyes—and bolder. He began visiting with other crows, possibly to learn how to caw. He also went to neighboring farms begging for handouts. Crow's panhandling was his undoing. Sometime in early autumn he went one farm too far, and someone shot him.

Crows have always been looked on as black scoundrels for destroying sprouted corn in order to eat the moist kernels. (In fact, blackbirds eat more corn than crows do.) Thanks to this and some other bad habits, the crow is a choice target for many farmers. Some people even think of the crow with its coal-black feathers as an omen of evil. Edgar Allan Poe's poem "The Raven" (referring to the crow's near kin and look-alike) did nothing to help matters—especially the lines "Take thy beak from out my heart, / and take thy form from off my door! / Quoth the raven, 'Nevermore.'"

In our part of Ohio, crows begin nest-building in late March and early April. Four or five eggs are laid. About the size of a banty's eggs, they are blue-green blotched with brown and black. When the eggs hatch in eighteen days, the adult crows become true predators as they hunt food for their growing young. Opportunists now, they pluck eggs and recently hatched young from the nests of many songbirds. Oftentimes in May, crows can be seen flying over hay fields with their black bills pointed toward the earth, on the lookout for bird nests. Suddenly the crow will wheel about and drop to the ground—and that's the end of another bird's nesting attempt.

Several springs ago while sowing oats, I watched a crow carry away the young from a well-concealed nest in the wheat field. I sent two loads from the twelve-gauge after the robber, but no feathers floated to earth.

Fed on a protein-rich diet, the young crows leave the nest after five weeks. Throughout the summer and early fall the crow family stays together. During this time the young become as proficient as their parents in finding food, which by now consists mainly of grains, insects, and mice.

Aside from man, crows have one main enemy: the great horned owl. Even so, they never pass up a chance to harass an owl—it seems to be a favorite pastime. If an owl is discovered in its daytime roost, reinforcements are called and the heckling begins. If the owl grows uneasy and flies to another part of the woods, the crows give merry chase until the owl finds a new perch. After a while, if the owl remains sitting, the brawl dies down to an occasional "caw" of half-hearted disgust.

The crows' hatred stems from the horned owl's nighttime habit of snatching roosting crows for a meal when rabbits and mice are scarce—in times of deep snow, for instance. Something that has long puzzled me is why great horned owls don't pluck incubating crows from their nests in April and May, a time when young owlets are demanding great amounts of food. Likewise, crows almost never mob incubating owls. It must be that the crows and owls have worked out a truce for the spring nesting season—a cease-fire in their war.

By late fall most crows migrate south for some distance, often congregating in immense flocks. However, at our farm a small band stays behind to watch over the winter woods, to heckle a few owls, and to wait for the manure spreader to bring their meals on wheels.

WEASEL

I was startled the other day to see a meadow vole (one of those fat little short-tailed mice that abound in meadows and fields) come charging out of the grass-covered ditch and dash across the road as fast as its stumpy legs could carry it. Before the sprinting vole had reached the safety of the opposite ditch, it was followed by two more of its kin. These, however, instead of racing across the road, made large half-circles and then ran back into the same ditch twenty feet down the road.

Meadow voles are seldom seen on roads. I can't recall ever seeing one D.O.R. (dead on the road). So what was the purpose of their wild pavement races? Maybe the voles were attending a survival school and were practicing predator-evasion skills to be able to outrun the fox and hawk and numerous other enemies that depend on them for winter food. Probably, though, a small predator, like a shrew or a weasel, had entered the underground labyrinth of vole tunnels and surprised the little rodents, which then exited in a hurry and were simply racing to save their lives.

I stopped and watched the spot where the meadow voles had emerged. Soon a small pointed nose poked through the grasses and two obsidian eyes glared at me—a weasel. No wonder the voles were scared silly. Of all their enemies, nothing alarms the mouse family as much as the weasel, because there is no place to hide from the long and slender killer. Where a vole goes, a weasel can follow. Occasionally a weasel will go on a rampage and kill much more than it needs for food. The voles are well aware of the weasel's nasty temperament.

Fortunately—for the voles, anyway—long-tailed weasels (*Mustela frenata*) are not very common around here. Their population tends to fluctuate greatly from year to year. Some winters I see almost no tracks in the snow of hunting weasels. A few winters later the small side-by-side tracks (leaping colons, : :) may again be common in and around brush piles and in weedy fields—wherever there are mice and rats and cottontail rabbits.

The long-tailed weasel is closely related to the ermine, or short-tailed weasel, of colder regions, which turns white in the wintertime. Both belong to the family of mustelids, which in this part of Ohio also includes the mink, otter, and skunk. Aside from the skunk, which is a heavyset plodder, most mustelids are long and slender, almost serpentine, and have short legs. They run, or rather leap, humpbacked, seeming to flow across the landscape.

Mustelids share another trait, and that is powerful scent glands—though none come close to the overwhelming potency of the skunk. The musk of the weasel and mink is similar and is released when the animal is threatened or excited. Unlike the strong, tear-inducing "oniony" musk of the skunk, the weasel's scent is much milder, more earthy and musty, an aroma as wild and elusive as its owner.

Weasels are rarely observed. I have seen fewer than a dozen in my lifetime, and some of those were D.O.R.'s. Two of the road kills I found were during the wintertime, and both showed an unusual amount of white fur in their normally brown coats. One was almost as white as an ermine. In most cases our winter weasels sport the same coats they do in summer: brown on top, white below, and with black-tipped tails.

Weasels have one litter of young annually. The four to six young are born in April or early May following a gestation period of around 280 days, though it can vary from 105 to 337 days. After mating in July and following a short period of development, the fertilized ovum is not implanted until the following spring, about twenty-five days before the young are born. This strategy of delayed implantation assures that the young are born when food is plentiful. A hay field in late May and June is a smorgasbord for a family of weasels.

Compared to most other mammals, weasels are born premature and don't open their eyes until they are five weeks old. At that time the mother begins to bring the young food from her field foraging. Gradually the young are weaned and switched to a carnivorous diet. By fall the young weasels are fully grown and hunting on their own, and the family disperses. There will be bloodletting in the tunnels of voledom.

The young weasels will be svelte and swift like their parents and will join the few other solitary predators that kill prey larger than themselves. Although they can take down a cottontail rabbit, voles and mice are their preferred fare. As cold months approach, the weasels will spend a large part of their time in the underground labyrinth of voledom, a place foreign to humankind but well traveled by the weasel.

WOOLLY WORMS

There's no denying it: the season's changing. The gold and red leaves of autumn are coming down in droves, opening up the landscape to reveal hills that were hidden by the lushness of summer. Only a few hardy insects still make music if the evenings are warm enough. The birds, too, sense the change, and many have followed their instincts southward. A recently arrived lone snow goose may have already flown several thousand miles from its summer home and is now spending time on our farm with a small flock of Canada geese that may stay around all winter if the weather remains mild. The pretty white goose is fattening up on corn before continuing its journey to the marshes along the Atlantic coast.

In a way it's sad to see the verdure of spring and summer and early fall come to an end. As William Cullen Bryant writes in *The Death of the Flowers*, "The melancholy days have come, the saddest of the year, Of wailing winds and naked woods, and meadows brown and sere."

It is hard to imagine that only a few months ago we sought shade away from the unrelenting heat of the sun. Now it seems that all creation can't get enough of the sun. The cows and the horses bed down in full sun; the dogs stretch out in its warmth. Snakes uncoil in its comfort. Groundhogs revel in its brightness. I remove my coat to it. Is there a longing, a hope, that in some way we can store the glorious heat and release it during the coming dark and barren months? I don't know, but I do know this period of pleasant and sunny weather is wonderful.

As many animals slow down and simply enjoy the Indian summer sun, the woolly bear caterpillars use it to move around. Woolly worms are always in a hurry. And I can't recall ever seeing as many of the brown-and-black caterpillars as there are this fall. They are everywhere—crawling cross-country through the lawn, climbing to the haymows, curled in the woodpile, bustling across the road.

It is on the roads where woolly worms often encounter tragedy. The other day I walked a hundred feet north from our mailbox to pick up a discarded Busch Lite carton. On the way back I counted a dozen squished woolly bears on the blacktop. In spite of the high mortality rate, at least a dozen more were making their way across the road—some going west and others east, like shoppers at a mall.

The woolly worm is the larval stage of the Isabella moth (*Isia isabella*), a small—its wingspan is one and one-half to two inches—pinkish-yellow moth that ranges throughout North America north almost to the Arctic Circle. Unlike many other caterpillars, which spin into cocoons, the woolly bear hibernates. It seeks shelter in stone walls and woodpiles, behind loose bark on trees, and beneath boards and logs, where it will curl up tightly in a fuzzy ball and sleep through the winter, impervious to the worst weather the season can throw at it.

The next spring the woolly bear will leave its winter home, find a plant to its liking—the plantain is its favorite—feed, spin into a cocoon, and then hatch out as an Isabella moth.

According to folklore, the woolly bear is a weather forecaster. It all depends, woolly-worm watchers claim, on the width of the brown segment that covers the caterpillar's middle. If it has a lot of black on its ends, causing the brown middle stripe to be narrow, the coming winter will be a tough one—long and severe. If the brown band is wide, the winter will be milder than usual.

Biologists, more soberly, point out that the bands vary from population to population. Some families of woolly bears simply have wider brown bands than their neighbors. Likewise, those that are brown, blond, or all-black belong to different species, the biologists claim.

I have never paid much attention to the woolly bear as a weather prophet because to me they look pretty much the same from year to year. Last week I stopped my bicycle on the road to protect a woolly worm from a car approaching from the rear. The speeding car turned out for me, thus missing the hustling caterpillar by a foot. But the rush of air blew the furry critter to the edge of the road, causing it to curl up in defense. Even to a woolly bear, life is full of surprises. Uncurling, the worm promptly headed in the opposite direction from the one it had been going.

I enjoy woolly bears for their exuberance: they celebrate the last warm days of autumn to the dregs.

WINTER SOLSTICE

By the calendar, the shortest day of the year has come and gone. The winter solstice occurred on the 22nd, when the year reached its nadir—that time when the sun stands still before slowly turning and beginning its climb upward in the sky, toward another spring and summer.

Winter actually begins long before the solstice. Botanists say the season starts when the average daily temperature falls below forty-three degrees Fahrenheit, the point at which plant growth stops and winter dormancy begins. The New England naturalist Hal Borland insisted that their winter began on the first full moon after the middle of November—which this year would have been December 6—the moon the Indians called the Cold Moon.

For farmers, winter begins when we move the cattle from pastures to the barn, which can be anywhere from mid-November to early December. Every farmer tries to graze as long as possible to save on winter feed. This year the cattle were moved indoors on November 11, a week or two earlier than usual; but it was necessary on account of a gale-driven rain that changed to snow.

While domestic animals have the luxury of being snugged in for the winter, with a feed supply that promises to last until spring, wild creatures must cope as best they can in the cold and snow. Some are well adapted to survive in this bitter weather, such as the snow bunting that was feeding on cracked grain with our local horned larks on the first day of winter. It and the larks seemed impervious to the wind and cold.

Unlike the bunting and other migratory birds, which travel thousands of miles south to more agreeable climates, mammals tend to stay in fairly small areas and tough the winter out. (Some ungulates do travel great distances from summer to winter ranges, such as the caribou in the arctic and Africa's wildebeest.) A few mammals hibernate during the cold and dark months. Right now the woodchuck, for example, is curled in a ball in its leaf- and grass-lined nest somewhere in the maze of its underground burrow. The nest is below the frost line, so the woodchuck remains comfortable living off the body fat it gained in the fall.

Raccoons, too, semi-hibernate, surviving on the energy of stored fat—fat gained from a summer and autumn of gluttonous living on sweet corn and chicken. Its frequent neighbor the opossum, though, is not so fortunate. An animal better adapted to the warmer climate south of the Mason-Dixon Line, the poor critter suffers if our northern winters are severe. The opossum can be a butterball in the fall, but by Christmastime its reserves are depleted and it has to eat.

The northeastern snowstorm earlier this week left a fine dusting of powdery snow over the upper barn floor. In among the numerous barn-cat tracks crisscrossing the floor the following morning was a set of possum footprints. Similar to the imprint of a human hand with its protruding thumb, these tracks trailed along the edge of the haymow to the cow-feed hopper, where the possum fed on spilled grain. From there the tracks led to a stack of straw bales, where it obviously has its winter den. Relative to its summer diet of bird eggs, carrion, and pokeberries, cow feed must seem pretty meager fare. I felt sorry for the hungry possum and left a handful of dog food by the feed hopper. The next morning every Golden Bit was gone.

In this season of short daylight hours, many people get the winter blues. Medical science calls the condition Seasonal Affective Disorder (SAD). The symptoms include mild depression, fatigue, increased sleep, and weight gain (that desire to hibernate?). The malaise can be corrected by exposure to bright lights, walking outdoors for at least thirty minutes each day, or Tucson.

This is also the holiday season: a celebration of a holy day, a time of reverence for life and the spiritual meanings implicit to it. I think of these beautiful lines in *The Book of Common Prayer:* "Oh Lord, support us all through the day long, until the shadows lengthen and evening comes, and the busy world is hushed, and the fever of life is over, and our work is done. Then in Thy mercy grant us a safe lodging, and a holy rest, and peace at last."

WEATHER LORE

No one seems to know exactly when or where the groundhog (or woodchuck) was elevated to the role of weather prophet. Some people are of the opinion that it all began in the 1800s in Punxsutawney, Pennsylvania, where the celebration of Groundhog Day has become a major annual event. The town even has a pet groundhog, Punxsutawney Phil, who wakens (or is awakened) from his winterlong slumber each February 2 to make a brief appearance and forecast the duration of winter.

Other people, however, claim that the belief in animals as weather prophets predates Punxsutawney Phil by centuries, going back to ancient times. In England, the badger was considered to be a weather forecaster. When the first English colonists settled along the Atlantic coast and found no badgers, they looked to the somewhat similar groundhog to take its place as a weather forecaster.

Regardless of its origins, Groundhog Day and February 2 are one and the same. On that day the groundhog is said to awaken from hibernation and venture forth from its burrow. If it sees its shadow, according to legend, it will retreat to its den and winter will linger for another six weeks. Should the weather be cloudy and the groundhog not see its shadow, it will end its sleep and winter's worst will be over.

I doubt whether many people have much faith in this often-proven-wrong legend. It would be more accurate to say that if the groundhog sees its shadow, winter will last another six weeks, whereas if the day is overcast and it doesn't see its shadow, winter will be over by mid-March!

The groundhog-as-prophet aside, discussing the weather is infinitely interesting to many people. It seems safe to say that comments about current weather patterns open more conversations—especially in rural areas—than any other topic. Countless times we have been greeted by friends, neighbors, and even strangers with "Sure is a nice day" or "Do you think the rain is over?" or "This wind sure cuts to the bone." Since it is such a neutral subject, one can hardly be accused of wrongdoing when discussing the weather.

We even tend to mark time by the occurrence of memorable weather events: for example, the Palm Sunday tornado of April 1965 that ripped through northern Indiana leaving a swath of destruction in its path; the Flood of 1969, when fourteen inches of rain were dumped on northeastern Ohio on July 4 and 5 causing destruction of property and loss of lives; and Hurricane Agnes in June 1972, which traveled up the eastern seaboard leaving mayhem in its wake and creating a counterclockwise flow of cold air and rain that pummeled the Midwest for two weeks. (In that massive storm, many purple martin landlords lost their entire colonies.)

Also memorable was the winter of 1976–77, the coldest in weather history for Ohio and much of the Great Lakes region. The following winter brought the Blizzard of 1978, in which moist air from the Gulf of Mexico combined with frigid Canadian air to roar northeastward at speeds up to 80 miles an hour, setting on January 26 the lowest barometric reading ever recorded in Ohio. Then, of course, there was the Drought of 1988. And 1990 was the wettest on record for Ohio, with almost sixty inches of rain. Yes, the weather seems to offer a never-ending parade of surprises.

Weather lore and sayings are almost as interesting as the weather itself. Lore has it that a month with a second full moon, or "blue moon," is generally colder than usual. The fact that this event occurs only once every two and one-half years gives rise to the saying "Once in a blue moon."

Many weather sayings do have a lot of truth in them, thanks to years of experience and observation by farmers and other people whose lives are centered around the weather. In Ohio, for example, the motto "Red sky at night, sailors' delight; red sky in the morning, sailors take warning" is quite accurate.

Shorter-term forecasters are bees: when they're all heading toward their hives, rain can be expected within thirty minutes.

The songs and activities of birds can also be indicators of a change in the weather. I have noticed that if birds are exceptionally active at the feeders late in the afternoon, there is a good chance of snow during the night or early the next day. I was told at a recent school meeting, as we stoked the old furnace, that a shower of sparks in the firebox is another sign of snow. Since I like snow, I'll gladly encourage dancing sparks.

One of the surest indicators of rain in the summertime that I've found is when the settlings in our livestock water trough rise to the surface. It likely has to do with a drop in the barometric pressure. Also in summer, clouds showing "mare's tails and mackerel scales" often indicate rain within forty-eight hours. The beautiful, feathery mare's-tail clouds are called cirrus; these, together with cirrocumulus and cirrostratus clouds, are the highest, often from four to eight miles up in the sky. Midlevel clouds are the altocumulus and altostratus, while low-level clouds—those dreary, all-day-rain clouds— are the stratus, nimbostratus, and stratocumulus. Cumulus clouds are the fluffy ones common on pleasant summer afternoons, marching across the sky like flocks of sheep.

Then there are cumulonimbus clouds—gigantic clouds that

roll their massive thunderheads thousands of feet into the warm and humid summer sky, forming violent storms. It was one of these great storms that broke the Drought of 1988. In an instant, as the rain came pouring down, the future of farming looked promising again.

Weather forecasting has developed into a science, with weather stations around the world and satellites aloft keeping an eye on approaching storms and measuring atmospheric pressure. With this technology, weather patterns can be fairly accurately predicted three to five days in advance. Farther ahead than that there is still a lot of guesswork involved. Maybe then we'll do best to look to moon haloes, the lowly woolly worm, and the *Old Farmer's Almanac* to discern what the future holds.

Humankind can send spacecraft to distant planets, split atoms, and splice genes, but we cannot stop a blizzard, tornado, or thunderstorm. We farmers live with the weather: we watch the clouds and monitor wind direction; we get caught in it; we lose crops and livestock to it—and yet, we have no notion or desire of ever mastering it.

Whether the drowsy old groundhog sees its shadow or not, as February ends and the earth tilts more toward the sun, we feel its warmth and dream of spring. The horned larks, my winter field companions, are also conscious of the growing length and intensity of daylight, and their soft lyrics float through the warming air. I hope to find their nests when sowing clover seed on the wheat ground. As Barry Lopez so beautifully writes in his book *Arctic Dreams:* "In a simple bow from the waist before the nest of the horned lark, you are able to stake your life, again, in what you dream."

THE FIELDS

EMERGENCE

Yesterday while I was rolling up fence wire I saw two Milbert's tortoise shell butterflies flying across the field. In the sixty-degree sunshine weather of mid-March, the colorful little butterflies seemed none the worse after enduring the long winter. They, too, must think that we are on winter's margin and are ready to get on with spring.

Sometimes I am astounded that any insects survive a hard winter, particularly those that don't burrow below frostline, like the tortoise shell. The hardy butterfly often crawls beneath a curling piece of bark on a tree and there lives through subzero temperatures, snow, ice, wind, and rain. All winter it doesn't eat and yet survives in fine fettle.

Since all insects are cold blooded, cool weather slows them down, and winter stops them in their tracks. In order to live through the cold season, when their development and activities cease, insects enter a resting stage called diapause. Monarch butterflies migrate to the mountains of Mexico for that stage of their lives, while tortoise shell and the mourning cloak butterflies stay and become dormant in our northern winters. However, on the first warm days of late winter they are out skating through the air in search of some early nectar or pollen.

Bees also live through the winter, but they do it in the warmth of a colony of their kin inside a beehive or a hollow tree. Feeding on stored honey, bees form a cluster whose center may be quite warm. By constantly moving from the outside edge of the cluster toward the center and then back out, all the bees have a chance of finding warmth.

Some insects, like the silkworm moths, live through the winter in their pupal stage, sheltered inside a tough silk-woven cocoon—unless, that is, a downy woodpecker decides to supplement its winter diet with the juice of a promethea or cecropia moth-to-be. The downy will peck a small hole through the cocoon to get at the larva. Its long bill serves as a straw to suck the life out of the worm. The luna and polyphemus moth caterpillars spin their cocoons on the ground and seldom fall victim to a woodpecker. In cold winters, a surprising number of silkworms perish. Although the cocoons are waterproof, they do not insulate the pupating larva from the cold.

A great number of insects prepare for winter by laying eggs in late summer and fall and then dying before the onset of cold weather. The praying mantis is a good example. In late summer the mantis lays its eggs in a tan frothy mass that when dry becomes as tough as plastic. By the end of October most adult mantids are dead.

On one of the fence posts, as I unclipped the wire, I found a mass of Carolina mantis eggs. The fifty to eighty eggs inside the egg case will begin to develop once the weather stays warm, and sometime in late spring the nymphs will hatch, disperse, and begin their life of devouring other insects. Mantids are virtually the only insects introduced accidentally to America that are beneficial to farmers and gardeners.

Another insect active now and beneficial to gardeners is the ladybug. We have a hazelnut tree near one of our gardens, and every autumn ladybugs congregate by the hundreds at its base, apparently spending the dark and cold months somewhere in the tree's root system. Today I checked and the small brightly colored beetles were up and about. Though very much alive, they are still not venturing far from their winter home in case cold weather returns.

Sometime in early spring the overwintering ladybugs will mate and begin laying their up to five hundred eggs, usually on the underside of leaves, over a two-month period. Soon after the young hatch they begin feeding on aphids and other small insects. Ladybug larvae consider the eggs of other insects a delicacy, especially those of the irksome Colorado potato beetle. An individual ladybug may consume five thousand aphids in its lifetime. Once the larva begins pupating, it remains quiet for a week to rearrange its body parts before emerging as an adult ladybug. As an adult, it will continue to eat aphids and eggs, though at a slower pace.

The colorful beetles have been showing up in nursery rhymes and children's stories for many generations. Swedish farmers call them the "Virgin Mary's Golden Hens," and to the Germans a ladybug is a *Marienkäfer* (Virgin Mary ladybird). I once saw a Volkswagon Beetle painted to look like a ladybug. Sue Hubbell writes in her wonderful book, *Broadsides from the Other Orders: A Book of Bugs*, that ladybugs are the pandas of the insect world, loved by humans universally.

RABBITS

I can't recall a year when spring was so eagerly awaited. After another week of brisk north winds and morning temperatures that dipped into the thirties, winter finally relinquished its hold. The wind shifted to the south, the mercury soared to the seventies, and it felt like spring at last.

It is amazing how swiftly spring rushes north with favorable winds and warmer temperatures. Crocuses in the flowerbeds and yellow coltsfoot along the roadsides, which had timidly tested the air a few times the past two weeks, now are fully opened to the sun. And the loveliest of all to me, the woodland hepaticas, are just starting to bloom.

New birds are showing up everywhere—vesper and savannah sparrows in the fields, chipping sparrows in the yard, purple martins in their houses, and last night two cliff swallows darted around the barn eaves checking out their mud homes from last year. The other day a tightly bunched flock of pectoral sandpipers turned and dipped over the plowed fields but didn't stop.

Unfortunately, there is also a downside to the unfolding of the season. Near the edge of the hay field there was evidence of foul play: some young cottontail rabbits will not be around to enjoy the heat and new clover of the returning spring. What caught my attention was the scattered fur that the female rabbit plucks from her body and uses for nest material. When I checked the hollow where the nest was I found it empty of young cottontails—the work of a predator.

But what predator I could only guess, because there are

many animals that will dine on young rabbits if the opportunity arises. It could have been a fox or raccoon or skunk or opossum or dog or feral house cat, or perhaps it was one of the numerous crows that course across the fields daily—though the widely scattered fur probably absolved the crow from guilt. Crows are neater. With their long black bills they pick out the young rabbits one by one without disturbing the nest.

Up until the time a young rabbit can outrun or outmaneuver an enemy, it depends on staying well hidden to preserve its skin. For that reason the mother will leave the brush piles and woodchuck burrows where she spent the winter and find a barren field to give birth to her three to eight young.

Several days before the young are born, the female, or doe, digs a hollow, often beneath or next to a tuft of grass, about the size of her body. Something that has always puzzled me is what she does with the excavated dirt, since I've never seen a mound of fresh soil near the nest. My guess is that the doe digs frantically and flings the soil ten to fifteen feet away from the nest to foil the army of predators, most of which have a superkeen sense of smell. A bungling opossum can find a nest of rabbits better than most predators if there is any giveaway of location at all, such as freshly dug soil. The opossum doesn't have that long pointy nose for merely cosmetic reasons.

The nest of young cottontails will be unattended during the daylight hours; its survival therefore depends on how well the doe camouflaged it, especially from flying predators. The doe spends the day hiding and resting in nearby cover. At night, she will visit the nest several times to nurse her young, with the last feeding just before daybreak. Even then, the youngsters will have to wait fourteen to sixteen hours before their next meal. While the mother is out in the open field she exposes herself to predators, especially the great horned owl,

61

which has its own youngsters, begging for food. It seems death comes from all directions for the unwary cottontail.

Soon after giving birth the female breeds again, and litter follows litter at approximately one-month intervals from spring through summer and into every fall. The females born in early spring will have litters of their own by late summer. Of the twenty-five to thirty offspring one female cottontail is capable of producing in a year, only four to eight will survive until November.

The number of rabbits surviving depends completely on their habitat, not on the number of predators pursuing them. In this part of the country, where there is ample food and water available for rabbits, the crucial factor is cover. If all fencerows are taken out, brush piles removed, roadsides sprayed, and cornfields sterilized clean of any weed, naturally the cottontail population will be low. But who gets blamed for there being so few rabbits? The great horned owl, red-tailed hawk, and the fox, of course.

FARMLAND SPARROWS

While working around the farm in the springtime one becomes somewhat accustomed to all the different bird songs. Not that the friendly chatter of the purple martins and the swallows or the lilting song of the orchard oriole goes unnoticed or becomes mundane. For the most part, though, it seems we listen to the whole chorus instead of the individual parts—until, that is, a new voice joins the crowd.

Last spring I was in the shop getting the corn planter ready for the field when a new bird song stopped me in midstride. It sounded like the far-off singing of a western meadowlark, a bird I'd been waiting for many years to visit our neighborhood. Quickly stepping outside I listened for at least five minutes. Nothing. Was it all my imagination?

Finally I went inside again, and had barely picked up the wrench when I heard the song again. Back outside, and . . . silence. This happened several more times before it occurred to me that I was probably spooking the bird whenever I left the shop.

All the while I was working I had noticed five or six white-crowned sparrows in an elderberry bush twenty-five or so feet from the doorway. The next time the bird sang I stayed inside and watched the sparrows. Sure enough, one had its head tilted back and was singing the mystery song. The melody was soft, giving the impression of being farther away, and several notes closely matched those of the western meadowlark's song. It was the first time I had heard a white-crowned sparrow sing.

The migrant white-crowned sparrow is, to me, the most handsome of the sparrows to be seen in our part of Ohio. With its black-and-white striped crown it lacks the drabness of most of the sparrow tribe, although its cousin the white-throated sparrow is almost as showy. The white-throated, too, has head stripes, as well as a white throat patch. And its song, which sounds like "Pure sweet Canada, Canada, Canada," is much more frequently heard during the spring migration than that of the white-crowned.

Sparrows belong to the finch family, a large family that includes buntings, grosbeaks, juncos, redpolls, and towhees. (The house sparrow, however, is in the weaver finch family.)

On the sparrow branch of the family tree, Roger Tory Peterson in *A Field Guide to the Birds of Eastern North America* shows twenty-six species. Out of these we get to see, and maybe hear, ten or twelve every spring and summer.

Some, like the white-crowned, white-throated, fox, Lincoln's, and American tree sparrows, we see only in winter or in passage. While the delightful birds may linger in Ohio for a spell, they will eventually migrate to the Hudson Bay country and on to the very edge of the arctic for the summer.

A number of sparrows, however, migrate to this part of the country for the nesting season. Right now the commonest sparrow in our fields is the savannah. Looking somewhat like a short-tailed, yellow-eye-striped version of the song sparrow, the savannah's flight is totally different. Today while spreading manure I watched at least three pairs as they playfully pursued their mates along the edge of the hay field. Flying stiff-winged, yet fluttering rapidly across the top of the hay, they would drop suddenly into the long grass, where they nest. Unfortunately, the savannah sparrow's song is on a frequency that my ears can barely pick up. So I just watch them sing.

Likewise, the grasshopper sparrow, also a nester in our fields, sings a song that suggests the chirp of a grasshopper. I can hear grasshoppers, but not these sparrows. When flushed the little sparrow flutters a short distance and drops back into the hay, like a miniature rail.

Another sparrow of the fields, and one that is easier to identify, is the vesper sparrow. It is easily recognized by its white outer tail feathers, which can be seen when it flies. And it sings a wonderful song, a melody that fits its home in the open country: spirited and free. Often its lyrics can still be heard in the twilight—hence its name, vesper sparrow.

The field sparrow is also a spirited songster. Beginning with a few slurred notes, the song gathers speed and ends in a trill. It is a familiar sound along fencerows. Contrary to its name, the field sparrow is more at home in overgrown fields and brushy fence lines than in tilled fields. It builds its nest on the ground or low in brushy cover such as multiflora roses.

In orchards and around buildings, song sparrows and chipping sparrows are the common residents. These two are probably the most widespread and, because of their habit of nesting near humans, the best known of the sparrows in eastern North America.

Wintering in the southern United States and in Latin America, the chipping sparrows arrive back in our area sometime in April. The small, trusting birds with their bright rufous caps are a joy to have around. We must have six pairs right around the house now. One pair has its nest in the sweet cherry tree, another in the blue spruce, and another in the juniper shrub at the end of the lane. Once the young hatch they wax fat on garden pests. As I have mentioned before, I take great pleasure in watching adult chipping sparrows diligently search the broccoli, cauliflower, and cabbage plants for pesky cabbage loopers. Chipping sparrows will raise several broods and stay around until autumn.

Our only year-round resident sparrow is the song sparrow. It sings throughout the year, but its spring song is prettier than its winter tune. Its favorite nesting place is along road and creek banks, where its grassy cup-shaped nest blends into last year's dead grasses.

In spite of the song sparrow's adeptness in hiding its nest, the brown-headed cowbird often finds it and lays its own egg in the nest, after first removing one of the song sparrow's eggs. Chipping sparrow nests are also frequent hosts for the cowbird's eggs. Occasionally we see a pair of chipping sparrows busily stuffing worms down the maw of a begging young cowbird that is already twice the size of its foster parents.

While the chipping sparrow's song is no more than the bird's name suggests—a chipping—the song sparrow is a much more accomplished vocalist. John James Audubon wrote concerning the song sparrow: "Although its attire is exceedingly plain, it is pleasing to hear." These mornings we waken to the song sparrow's early music outside the bedroom window. It's a nice way to start the day.

HAY FIELD BESTIARY

It always surprises me how quickly hay fields abound with new life once regrowth begins in the spring. Migrant birds arrive, pair off, and begin nesting. Mammals move in from the edges. Soon the fields ring with bird song and bustle with the activities of all the new inhabitants.

To me, a mixed grass-and-legume hay field is an eastern version of the lush midwestern prairie. Many of the animals, birds, and insects here are the same as those inhabiting native prairies. Grassland birds, unlike their woodland cousins, often sing on the wing. And the songs of some, like the meadowlark and bobolink, are loud enough to carry well on the wind and across the great distances of open spaces. Unfortunately, the field's richness of life peaks around mid-June, right at the time the hay needs to be cut.

I was cutting the first round of hay when a red fox left the field and headed for the security of the fencerow. I was happy to see the fox, a pup, which means a litter was raised nearby. About a month ago I had found a partially eaten muskrat at the edge of the hay field, a killing that looked like the work of a family of red foxes. The pair of foxes whose tracks crisscrossed the fields in last winter's snow apparently decided to stay and raise their family. Along the fence line there are at least a dozen woodchuck burrows; any one could be the home of the foxes.

I greatly admire the red fox, for its grace and beauty and its ability to survive in the proximity of humans. A family of red foxes on the farm makes it a better place to live.

Soon after I saw the fox several half-grown cottontail rabbits left the hay field, going in the opposite direction of the fox. The fox may have been stalking the rabbits when I flushed it out. Indeed, the field is a premier stalking arena: the shrew stalks the beetles and earthworms; the weasel stalks the shrew; the fox stalks the voles and cottontails; the red-tailed hawk watches for weasels, voles, cottontails, and shrews; the crow searches for the eggs and young of red-winged blackbirds—as does the black rat snake—and the Cooper's hawk darts out from the cover of the woods to snatch a bobolink or redwing or horned lark. The skilled eat. Fortunately, there is an abundance of life.

One evening I saw a weasel out for an early hunt. It was headed my way, so I remained motionless. Every few lopes it would stop and sniff the air (did it smell a mouse or was it me?) but then kept coming closer. The weasel's back was grayish brown and the underside white. It was slender and only around ten inches long, and it ran humpbacked. I saw spots of blood on its nose as it passed between my legs.

The red-winged blackbirds nest early and most of their young are already flying. Likewise with the savannah sparrows: their young are everywhere, clinging to stalks of weeds and grass. But the bobolinks are late again; I haven't seen any flying young.

Last evening as I was coming home from raking hay in our far field, I passed the uncut mixed-hay field. It was just before sunset, at the time the bobolinks are at their finest, and I counted sixteen males zigzagging across the field, chasing mates and competitors, and singing their lively songs. I paused to listen and to watch the birds, and tried to envision what it must have been like when the first Europeans saw the vast expanse of the American prairie—a band of grass six hundred miles across and extending a thousand miles from north to south. How many millions of bobolinks were in those virgin grasslands?

We'll wait to cut that field. Give the bobolinks a week, and their young may be flying.

Another animal I saw while mowing hay this week was a white-tailed deer. It had bedded down along the edge of the field, but when I approached it spooked and left. The deer, a buck with antlers in velvet, was wearing its reddish-brown summer coat, so different from the drab gray of winter.

Of course, there are the usual woodchucks in the hay field. In fact, without the woodchuck there would be less life altogether in the hay field. The red foxes, for one, wouldn't have raised their family here if it hadn't been for the woodchuck's burrows. The cottontails and weasels also use the burrows. Even the pair of bobwhite quail that lives in the hay field may use the woodchuck's den in the wintertime to escape freezing rains. For many grassland creatures, the woodchuck's burrows are crucial for surviving the perils of predation and fierce weather. Long live the grizzled hay-eating rodents.

THE KILLDEER

I had just started cultivating a row of corn in the middle of the field when a killdeer fluttered out from in front of the team. Pretending it had a broken wing, the bird spread its rust-colored tail and flapped cross the ground while loudly calling, "Killdeah, killdeah." Even though the killdeer acted and sounded as if it were seriously injured, I knew it was all a show to draw me away from its nest.

The nest, if such it can be called, was just to the side of the row of corn. It was easy for the horses to straddle it, and I raised the cultivator, thus saving the eggs. Traveling maybe a hundred feet beyond the nest I stopped and watched. Because the temperature was only around fifty degrees Fahrenheit, I guessed the killdeer would soon return to its duties of incubating. (The male and female are identical in appearance and share in tending the eggs.) Running a few feet, the killdeer would stop and crouch, bob a few times, then continue toward the nest. Once it got there it sat on the four eggs, folded its long, spindly legs, fluffed out its feathers, wiggled from side to side several times, and resumed incubating. As I approached on the next round of cultivating, the bird left the nest for only a short time; then after about the third round, when it seemed to realize I would do it no harm, it stayed on the eggs as I passed nearby.

A member of the plover family, the killdeer is probably the best known of all North American shorebirds. It is easy to identify: gray-brown above with a rufous or orange rump and tail, and white below, with long straw-colored legs. The white underparts are accented with two black bands across its chest.

Found widely over much of Canada and almost everywhere in the United States during the summer, the killdeer has adjusted well to civilization. So well, in fact, that the strikingly marked bird will not hesitate to nest near people in gardens, tilled fields, driveways, parking lots, and even flat gravel-covered roofs of large buildings. With the exception of rooftops—which probably don't appear as roofs to the killdeer—it always nests on the ground like all other shorebirds.

Hollowing out a slight depression in the ground, the killdeer may add some pebbles, dried shreds of corn stalks, or whatever is available, and then it lays its four buff-with-bold-black-and-brown blotched eggs. The large eggs' pointed ends are always toward the center of the nest, forming an almost perfect square. Maybe that is why she seldom lays three or five eggs, which would seem to unbalance the clutch.

Since the killdeer's young are precocial, meaning they are covered with down and leave the nest soon after hatching, the eggs are much larger than, say, those of a robin, a similar-sized bird. (A robin's young, called altricial, are born blind and bare and need to be fed in the nest for close to two weeks.) The killdeer eggs require a longer incubation period: twenty-four days compared to thirteen days for the robin.

Throughout the long incubation the killdeer depends totally on camouflage for protection from predators such as hawks and owls. Should a four-legged predator like a dog, skunk, or opossum find the nesting bird, it will feign injury to draw the animal away from the eggs.

Once the chicks begin to hatch, the adult birds are especially protective. Calling in alarm, wing dragging, tail spreading, they can convince almost any creature to follow them away from the vicinity of the nest. As soon as the young have hatched, but before they are dry and ready to leave, the parents dispose of the eggshells by carrying them off or eating them, lest the shiny insides of the shells attract the sharp eyes of a cruising crow.

Occasionally killdeer nest together in small colonies. A friend of mine related how a person working at the local brick-yard found four pairs nesting nearby. Observing them almost daily, he was amazed when all four clutches hatched within a short time of each other.

Upon leaving the nest, the killdeer chicks—now dry and resembling mottled brown cottonballs on matchstick legs—will have to find their own food. Of course, the parents will lead them to areas of good foraging, usually pastures where insect life abounds. The killdeer on our farm like to feed in a cornfield where grubs, worms, and slugs have been brought to the surface by recent cultivation.

For the first week or two of their young lives the chicks will freeze when danger threatens. With their earth-tone coloring, the young are virtually impossible to find when motionless. Between two weeks of age and the time they begin to fly at twenty-five days, they depend on their long legs to escape from enemies. The four young dashing in four directions, along with the adult's broken-wing act, will confuse any attacker long enough for the birds to reach cover.

Usually a pair raises only one brood of young. Sometimes we see young killdeer as late as July, probably the result of a second nesting after the first clutch was destroyed. The first nest we found this spring was in early April. I was spreading manure in the heifer pasture when a killdeer suddenly flopped away from the spreader and team. The nest was easy to find: it was smack in the middle of a well-rotted cow pie. A few broken pieces of weathered weed stalks were spread around the pie to help in hiding the blotchy eggs.

72

As autumn approaches, the killdeer begin a leisurely south-ward movement. In mid to late fall flocks of twenty to thirty are common in our pasture field. In mild winters some of these hardy plovers may linger into early January. Two years ago on our Christmas bird count we found twenty-one of the handsome birds in a spring-fed wetland behind a barn.

Although some killdeer migrate as far as South America, many don't make it out of the United States and will over-winter in the southern coastal regions. Then sometime in late February or early March, when a warm Gulf breeze brings us a touch of spring, we hear the glad call of the first kill-deer as it searches for a wet spot in the pasture field.

In the excitement of the spring bird migration one seldom hears the killdeer mentioned. It's too common, a ho-hum, taken-for-granted bird. But while cultivating corn we have the killdeer for our companion. And prettier company would be hard to come by.

DOG DAYS

Sultry afternoons, cumulus clouds roiling upward along the western horizon, the mutter of distant thunder, the darkening sky dividing to the north, and to the south giving Wooster and Charm their timely rains, while we swelter in stifling heat. Typical weather of the Dog Days, which, according to the almanac, began earlier this week.

The Dog Days are named after Sirius, the Dog Star—the brightest star in the sky, shining from the throat of the Great Dog (the constellation Canis Major), who stands at Orion's heel as he gazes at the Seven Sisters. Sirius, in Greek, means glowing. The star rises and sets with the sun from early July through mid-August.

We did get rain—three inches over the past two weeks, breaking the drought of late spring. Fields of corn, which looked like fields of pineapples before the rains, were lush and green and chest high by the Fourth of July. Such luxuriance is a thing of great beauty to farmers who are buying grain because of last summer's drought.

It is at this time of the year that the countryside reaches its peak of splendor. Before the corn tassels it appears almost tropical in its deep green lushness, its richness accented by the light-green-with-tinge-of-yellow oats, along with the varying greens of meadows and second-crop hay fields. But what really gives color and balance to the variety of the fields is the ripening wheat—at the time it is cut with the binders and set into shocks, before it fades to dead ripe and still is glowing, golden bronze.

Even though fewer acres of wheat are being planted locally as the shift toward corn and alfalfa continues, my hope is that enough farmers will still put out wheat to add a golden touch to early July.

It seems the field birds were waiting for wheat shocks to perch on and proclaim to everything within hearing that these soft, hazy evenings of the Dog Days are something worth singing about. All spring we had been listening for the vesper sparrows without any luck. It wasn't until the other evening that several were singing their lively songs from the top of wheat shocks. The next morning I heard them again. From the far end of the field a bobwhite whistled his name, and a few lingering bobolinks contributed their cheerful notes.

Even though the musical *plinks!* of the young bobolinks as they prepare to migrate already suggest a waning of the season, the heart of summer is still ahead of us. It is at this time, before the birds quietly depart, that I like to pause to take inventory of the natural world.

The first of the young purple martins are flying with their parents seeking and feeding on winged insects. So are the young barn swallows in the milking stable. Already graceful, they skim low over the fields in pursuit of their own food. The parents have relined the nest with new white feathers, and the female is incubating another clutch of five eggs.

A pair of bluebirds are feeding a second brood, six this time, in the box by the big garden. A house wren is busy stuffing the unused bird boxes around the orchard with sticks, making music all the while. Cedar waxwings ate all the Juneberries; robins got most of the few sweet cherries. Monarch butterflies are everywhere. Today the first great spangled fritillary of the summer visited the orange flowers of the butterfly weed in the garden.

Milkweed blossoms are perfuming the evening air along the roadsides, while along the creek the warm air is sweet with the scents of mint and meadow roses. Wild raspberries are ripening; they will be shared with the catbirds.

Summer is right on schedule.

SUMMER BOUNTY

As July merges with August the heat and humidity of the Dog Days reach their peak. And so does the summer's farmwork. The threshing, second cutting of hay, and wheat stubble and pasture mowing keep us from spending much time in the woods. Aside, that is, from venturing out for wild berries.

It is partly because it provides a break in the farmwork that I enjoy picking blackberries so much. Regardless of how busy we are, when the blackberries are filled with sun-ripened sweetness we find time—maybe only a few hours or an evening—and head for the woods.

Last year I went by myself. I had sprayed an insecticide on our alfalfa in the morning, something I seldom do. But when one gets as desperate for hay as we were in last summer's drought, one tends to do desperate things. The second-cutting hay had yielded only one-sixth of a normal year's output, and although the third crop came on nicely when it finally started to rain, so did the crop-damaging potato leafhoppers. I read the insecticide label: "Do not enter field for four days following application. Do not pasture for ten days. Toxic to bees. Wear long-sleeved shirt and boots." My heart said no, but my head said yes. There was no white clover or other flowers in the field, which meant there were no bees or butterflies. So I sprayed.

Doing something unpleasant left me with the desire for a change of scenery, so I headed for our favorite blackberry patch. The thicket is located near the center of a wilderness of thorn apples, wild apples, joe-pye weed, and a few multiflora roses—through which I was struggling when a catbird told me, somewhat halfheartedly, to go on home and forget it. I ignored its scolding and started picking the jumbo berries. As dry as it was last summer, the berries were as big around as my thumb, and half as long. Growing in the shade of young trees, many of the canes were bent over from the weight of the sweet fruits.

Even though the temperature was near ninety degrees, it was pleasant in the untethered old field and the afternoon passed swiftly as I moved from cane to cane filling my pail. A white admiral butterfly kept me company all the while I was there. It would flit ahead and sip the sweet juice from the ripest berries, usually the one on the tip of the cluster. When I approached the pretty insect would move to the next patch.

Besides the catbird there were few birds calling. An indigo bunting sang several refrains of its lively song but then gave in to the heat and rested. A cicada was more appreciative of the heat. Its raspy rising and fading buzz sounded most of the time I was there. When my two-gallon pail was filled to the brim I went home, and we had sugared blackberries with milk for supper.

Blackberries belong to the *Rubus* genus and, along with the closely related dewberry, are easily the most valuable wild fruit crop in America. (Blackberries have upright canes, while dewberries have trailing vines.) The blackberry can vary greatly even in the same general area. Some ripen early with small, seedy, and tart fruits, while others several hundred feet away may ripen a few weeks or even a month later with plump, sweet berries and few seeds. The ones we depend on are of the latter variety. They ripen to an evenness we have seldom found in other blackberries. Unfortunately, this superior strain will be lost in a year or two to the encroaching woods.

Around six years ago I transplanted ten of these plants to our orchard. The small fruits, however, bore little resemblance to their parent stock. What went wrong? One difference was that the transplants were in full sun, whereas the wild ones were in partial shade. Or maybe they need to be serenaded by the yellow-breasted chats and yellowthroats and indigo buntings and catbirds in order to bear full, juicy fruit.

Blackberries can be eaten as fresh fruit with sugar and milk or cream, as we did for supper, or in many other ways. They make superb jellies, jams (though somewhat seedy), pies, and cobblers. Our preferred breakfast drink in the winter months is blackberry juice. My wife makes this delicious beverage by taking a two-quart mason jar and adding one and a half cups of washed berries and one cup of white sugar. She then adds enough boiling water to cover the sugar and berries. After the sugar is dissolved the jar is filled with water and cold-packed in a boiling water bath for ten minutes. When a jar is opened in the wintertime and served chilled from the fruit cellar, I can almost hear the catbird scold.

The wild raspberry is the same genus as the blackberry and is fully as tasty as the tame variety. Smaller than the cultivated raspberry and not nearly as plentiful around here as the blackberry, the wild black raspberry is a real treat for us. The ones we gather are canned in a light syrup to be used for pies, and in good years, when there's a surplus, they end up in jam or as an ice cream topping.

Other wild berries that we use for pies and preserves are the elderberry and wineberry. The elderberry has been found to be one of nature's richest sources of vitamin C. Plentiful and easy to gather, the elderberry makes an excellent jelly. Since elderberries lack acid and are a bit bland, lemon juice is usually added to pies and jellies to give extra zest.

Almost all the wineberries we find are along roadsides. Looking somewhat like a red raspberry, the wineberry develops within a husk that opens only when the fruit is fully ripe. The red berries do not need lemon juice for tang because they have a sprite tartness themselves. They make a pretty and delicious reddish jam.

Wild strawberries are the rarest of the wild fruits in this part of the country—at least to me they are. The most of the tasty morsels I've ever found was a handful. Not nearly enough for strawberry shortcake or pie or jam. This isn't so in all parts of the country. Last year I received a letter from a friend in Meyersdale, Pennsylvania: "I have certainly enjoyed the last weeks," she wrote, "when I could go and pick wild strawberries. I picked 40 quarts so far. . . . "

FIREFLY NIGHTS

Dusk was fading into full darkness as we reached the end of the field and set the last bundles of wheat into shocks. Even though the heat of the day had lasted into the evening, the air was pleasant as my wife and I and the children walked down the field lane toward the house.

Ahead of us in the western sky the planets Venus, Jupiter, and Mars were together for the first time since the Boston Tea Party in the 1700s. This is an occurrence we will not see again in our lifetime; astronomers tell us that the next celestial reunion of these three planets is scheduled for the year 2250 or thereabouts.

On earth, though, an event was taking place that was almost equally spectacular. It occurs nightly from late spring through early summer as hundreds of fireflies rise from the hay and oat fields and from the meadows. Their lights of yellow and greenish yellow were brilliant against the darkness of the woods. We stopped to watch the show. At times the flashes seemed to be at random; then, as more fireflies took wing, they flashed almost in unison. Soon the night was twinkling with, to use a once-popular expression, "a thousand points of light."

With all the sunshine and heat we have had this spring and summer (May having been the warmest on record for Ohio), fireflies and other insects are especially abundant. Fireflies are sometimes called lightning bugs or, in our Pennsylvania-German dialect, "Blitzkäfer." They are, however, neither flies nor bugs but soft-bodied beetles in the family Lampyridae (from the Greek word *lampein*, meaning "to shine").

In the eastern United States two species of fireflies commonly occur. The Pyralis firefly (*Photinus pyralis*), which ranges westward to the Rockies, is the one that flashes the familiar yellow J-shaped signal. Flying in an undulating pattern, the male begins to light up just before he reaches the low point of his flight, maybe only several feet from the ground. Then for the duration of the flash he rises. This rising flash can give the impression that a whole field of fireflies in the twilight is taking flight. If we pay close attention, though, we see that the magical beetles never do fly very high.

Because the female usually stays on or near the ground, the male flies low so she can catch his signal. If she likes what she sees and responds several seconds later with a half-second signal, the male will continue to flash and move toward her. If the female again returns the compliment, the male will land and search her out.

The other firefly we commonly see is the Pennsylvania firefly (*Photuris pennsylvanicus*). Ranging from the East Coast westward to Texas and up into Manitoba, it is a trifle bigger than the Pyralis firefly and flashes a different signal of a more greenish-yellow light.

Interestingly, the female Pennsylvania firefly may mimic the mating signal of the Pyralis firefly, and when a male of that species approaches her, she eats him. Her trickery usually does not work on the first try. As many as a dozen Pryalis males may fly close to her false signal and then veer away before one lands and ends up as her main meal.

The luminous organs of fireflies are complex structures and have intrigued humans for many centuries. Aristotle, the Greek philosopher, wrote about them, and so did Pliny, the Roman author. Pliny's belief that fireflies turn their light on and off by opening and closing their wings was accepted and passed on for many centuries.

It was not until the late 1880s that a scientist came up with a name for the firefly's magic. Raphael Dubois, a Frenchman, discovered that the luminous organ on a firefly contains a fatty substance that, when exposed to air, quickly oxidizes and produces light. He named the substance "luciferin" (from the Latin word *lucifer*, meaning light-bearing).

When a firefly admits air through tiny tubes to its tail, the luciferin—in combination with luciferase, an enzyme, and several other chemicals—rapidly oxidizes and releases energy as light. The light given off is unique in being cold. Almost 100 percent of the energy produced is light—a feat that humans have never been able to accomplish. (When we shine our flashlight in search of female fireflies, or a neighbor switches on his electric lights, or we light our barn lantern, 90 percent of the energy is given off as heat and only 10 percent as light.)

Once the fireflies have mated, the female will lay eggs for a couple of days, on or just under the surface of damp soil. In about four weeks they will hatch and the larvae will begin to feed; they continue feeding until they have burrowed well underground for the winter.

Firefly larvae are predators and beneficial to farmers and gardeners, since they eat slugs, snails, mites, and other soil pests. Some ecologists think that numerous firefly larvae in the soil may be crucial in controlling slugs: the dramatic increase in the slug population in recent years, they suggest, may coincide with the increase in the use of soil insecticides, which kill firefly larvae and other enemies of the slimy slugs.

Like their parents, firefly larvae posses the power of light and hence are called glowworms. Their lighting ability puzzles some scientists, since the glowworm obviously does not light up to attract a mate. Why does it glow?

I have found that the best time to locate glowworms is on warm, late-fall nights when they are still feeding on the surface. I can remember going along coon hunting as a boy; while the hounds cold-trailed, I would look for glowworms, usually around wet spots or springs.

It is thought that firefly larvae stay in the soil until their third spring before pupating and hatching as adults. In our regularly rotated fields, most fireflies emerge from the oat fields. In mid-June we helped a neighbor put up hay. When we left his farm at dusk and passed the oat fields, thousands of fireflies were flying up and showing their mysterious lights in the warm, sultry evening. It was a show comparable to the Perseid meteor shower of August.

Scientists may be correct in saying that fireflies sparkle the night with their winking lights solely to attract mates, but I like to think that the little beetles do it at least partly for the enjoyment of us summer-evening porch sitters.

WEEDS

Ralph Waldo Emerson wrote that a weed is a plant whose virtues have not yet been discovered. James Lowell thought a weed is no more than a flower in disguise. I was thinking of those words of wisdom as I walked through our hay field yesterday and noticed the many spikes of moth mullein towering above the hay.

Depending on where moth mullein is found growing it may be looked at as a wildflower, but in a hay field it comes down on the side of a weed. Even if its white, or sometimes yellow, five-petaled flowers add a touch of brightness to the pink and purple flowering legumes, and even if it is visited by many different kinds of butterflies, it is still a weed. On dewy mornings is when moth mullein is at its prettiest; then its showy blossoms are at their peak of freshness. As the sun climbs higher into the sky and the temperature soars, the flowers close up to conserve moisture, appearing wilted.

What never ceases to amaze me is how well "weedy" wildflowers do in times of drought. I found out why last evening when I moved some fence in the hay pasture. The single- or double-stalked moth mulleins that were cut with the first-crop hay had now sprouted four to six stalks several feet tall, filled with buds, flowers, and seedpods. The mulleins seemed to leer at me. So out of spite, I began pulling them out of the ground.

Mulleins have a taproot that usually breaks off five inches or so below the surface of the dirt. One plant, however, surrendered its entire taproot, if somewhat reluctantly. I was so intrigued by the plant's tenacity that I took it home and measured the root. It was thirty-seven inches long! No wonder droughts are merely a minor annoyance to the moth mullein.

Moth mullein belongs to the snapdragon family and, according to the Peterson guide, is an alien. It likely hitched a ride to North America in the crop seeds that the European settlers brought along. So did many of the other weeds that cause problems in tilled fields and gardens: lamb's quarter, pigweed, purslane, bindweed, and the ragweeds all originally came from somewhere else.

Maybe it is as Emerson said, we simply haven't discovered these weeds' virtues. Take the common ragweed, for example, a weed that blooms from August until the first frost. This plant produces an abundance of fine air-borne pollen that every hay fever sufferer knows about. Surely such people in their teary-eyed sniffling agony wonder what good ragwood could possibly serve. But then there's the common redpoll, a colorful sparrow-sized bird from the arctic that only rarely travels this far south in great numbers; the redpoll believes that the common ragweed is God's gift to their kind.

Last winter the redpolls visited our neighborhood. Driven south by severe weather, the delightful little birds fed almost solely on ragweed seeds in last summer's wheat fields. In tight flocks of fifty to seventy-five birds, the redpolls could be fairly closely approached before they would take wing and fly to another part of the field to find more nutritious morsels. The snow was littered with the shells of seeds, seeds that supplied the energy for the redpolls to return to the arctic—and seeds that, thanks to the redpoll, will not be around to sprout, grow, and bloom and cause discomfort this summer. The plant that caused pain in August brought pleasure in January.

Ragweed seeds also are the preferred winter fare for the

bobwhite quail. The quail, however, have been in steady decline since the introduction of the herbicide 2,4-D sometime in the late 1940s, which laid low the ragweeds in corn. As my neighbor many times has said, "Before herbicides, only the good farmers had clean corn. Now anyone who wants to pay the price can have ragweed-free corn."

Maybe instead of looking at weed control we should consider weed prevention. The redpolls know all about it.

SNAKES ALIVE

"There's a snake in the garden!"

Those frantic words demand swift action on my part because a hoe, to a snake, is a lethal weapon. Many harmless garter snakes have been chopped to smithereens by frightened hoe-wielding gardeners.

This snake, a fair-sized garter maybe thirty inches long, was more fortunate. While my wife is not about to make a pet out of a snake, she will tolerate its presence in the garden. She hopes it will eat the mice and moles that tunnel beneath the hay mulch. I worry for the toads in the garden, though, which lap up vegetable-damaging insects and slugs at night. Garter snakes love to eat toads. A friend of mine once "rescued" a half-swallowed toad from the mouth of a garter snake, only to discover that the snake's powerful digestive juices had already dissolved the toad's legs.

Snakes must rank right near the top of the "most loathed list" of all the creatures on earth. After all, wasn't it the serpent, that slinky, deceiving snake, that tempted Eve in the Garden to pick the forbidden fruit, an act that then brought all sorts of grief (weeds and sweat and pain) on her descendants? Humankind has been beating the snake into the ground ever since for that deception—or so it seems.

Nothing in nature has aroused superstitions and myth like the snake has, particularly in rural areas. Every countryman has a favorite snake story or two. A recurring yarn is the one of a swimmer in a local lake getting caught in a tangle of water moccasins and dying within minutes. (In fact, the poisonous water moccasin or cottonmouth ranges no farther north than southern Virginia.)

Hearing all these tantalizingly scary snake stories as a boy is probably why I developed an affinity for the shy reptiles. Plus my grade school naturalist-teacher expounded the value of snakes, saying that they were very much a part of the natural world and should not be killed.

Because snakes are cold blooded, in the spring and fall they seek the sun to absorb its heat, but now in this overbearing heat of August they seek only shade. The other day while I was turning oat shocks to speed up their drying, I found two garter snakes coiled comfortably away from the beating-down sun. Underneath the shocks it was cool and moist and the field mice were abundant. What more could a snake desire but to sleep in a dining room well stocked with mice?

There are three poisonous snakes in Ohio: the timber rattler, found in small isolated colonies in southern Ohio; the northern copperhead, widely scattered throughout the southeastern part of the state; and the eastern massusauga, a small rattlesnake found in the wet prairies, bogs, and swamps of northwestern Ohio. No poisonous snakes frequent our part of the state, though occasionally a massusauga, or swamp rattler, is spotted in the wetlands along the Killbuck.

We have found five species of snakes here on our farm. Besides the common garter snake, the northern water snake is regularly seen along the creek, especially in the spring when they sun themselves on piles of driftwood. Only rarely do I find an eastern ribbon snake, which can easily be confused with the similar-looking garter snake. And once our daughter found an eastern smooth green snake in our woods. The dainty light-green snake blends so well with the summer foliage that it is seldom seen.

The fifth species we sometimes encounter is the black rat snake or black snake. It is Ohio's largest snake, commonly between four and six feet long, though Guy Denny writes in *Ohio's Reptiles* that the black snake may grow in excess of eight feet. Of course, tales abound of ten-to-twelve-foot-long black snakes, and they continue to grow in the storyteller's imagination. Unfortunately, black snakes are becoming rare in the tilled parts of the state. I know of two denning places where the black snakes, and possibly other species, go underground for the winter. One is in the Killbuck Marsh Wildlife Area. On warm days in late October two or three of the large and by then sluggish snakes can be seen loosely looped through the branches of shrubs like black garden hoses, soaking up the last of the season's sun before heading underground where the temperature is fifty degrees throughout the winter.

The latest wild snake story: the Division of Wildlife is releasing rattlesnakes to control the wild turkey population. Apparently timber rattlers eat turkey eggs. But the part I like is how the deadly snakes are released: they are dropped from helicopters in helium-filled balloons. So keep your eye on the sky.

STARLINGS

I must admit, I don't really love the starling. Admire the brassy bird, yes, but love, not quite. Last week, something happened that caused me to admire the starling even more. Actually, *Sturnus vulgaris* redeemed itself by doing such a good deed that I feel guilty for disliking the bossy immigrant at other times of the year.

This was a great summer for grasshoppers. They hatched early, probably because June was unusually warm, and by the time we mowed the second cutting of hay, grasshoppers had amassed by the thousands. Only half an inch long and a pleasing shade of light green, the little hoppers stayed away from the mowing machine; then, when the hay was put away, they moved to the potato patch next door.

The grasshoppers waxed fat on the leaves of the potatoes and on the new growth of hay and by last week had grown and molted several times and could fly. When we mowed the wheat-stubble field there were swarms of grasshoppers, now fully grown and winged.

Although the grasshoppers were able to fly, their guidance system left a lot to be desired. When I walked downwind to check the beehives in the orchard, a cloud of grasshoppers teemed ahead of me. Pushed by the tailwind, they didn't turn out for the hives but smashed into the boxes, bouncing off like rocks off a barn wall. After I left, the grasshoppers that weren't stunned by their run-in with the hives slowly worked their way back toward the field with short flights and long hops.

As a rule, grasshoppers don't do much agricultural damage here in the East, but I still worried: those tens of thousands of critters had to eat something. Most likely, I thought, the new seeding of hay was serving as their salad bar.

The next day a small flock of starlings visited the field to feed on the abundance of grasshoppers. Each day the flock grew bigger. They must have brought their friends until there were at least two thousand starlings. I can't describe the sensation I felt as I stood on the edge of the field watching that great assemblage of birds glean out those grasshoppers. No effort at all was required on my part, and yet it was so efficient.

The starling is a remarkably adaptive bird. The black-with-speckles-of-yellow bird, quite handsome in winter and during the breeding season (right now they have molted to a grayish brown), makes itself at home almost anywhere. Brought over from Europe and released in New York City in 1890, the starling took off and by the 1950s had colonized most of North America.

Its aggressiveness toward native birds is why many people hate the starling. Anyone who has a colony of purple martins knows the persistence of starlings in the spring when a pair is looking for a nesting site.

Since starlings are cavity nesters, woodpeckers especially have a tough time with the newcomers. As soon as a pair of woodpeckers excavates a new nesting hole, a starling couple arrives to take it over.

In the underside of a limb high on the maple tree by our house is an old woodpecker nesting cavity. Every spring starlings attempt to nest, despite our various efforts to deter them. Each time, though, the starlings win out and raise a brood. As soon as the young have fledged, they and their parents leave. By midsummer, masses of starlings from all around, begin to congregate to eat grasshoppers and other tasty treats.

Yesterday I walked through the wheat-stubble field, and where a week ago there were thousands of grasshoppers, I could not find a single one.

As you head south, *Sturnus vulgaris,* bon voyage.

PREDATOR AND PREY

The starlings are still around, lingering in large flocks in the almost-perfect weather. Now, instead of feasting on grasshoppers, they are entertaining us—unintentionally, of course. While I was plowing the other day, two distinct flocks kept me company. One was a mixed flock of brown-headed cowbirds, common grackles, and starlings. The other and larger flock was almost all starlings.

They would feed in the field, some on morsels exposed by the plow and the rest on hopping insects in the unplowed part of the field. When I got too near with the plow, the flock would take wing and fly off in search of a red-tailed hawk or some other not-too-dangerous raptor to pester. Starlings are swift and powerful flyers, and to watch the flock twist and turn in unison as it mobs a soaring hawk in the clear September sky is to watch grace in action.

I was working on the plow at the end of the field and wasn't paying attention to the starlings when they returned from their high-altitude concert. Suddenly there was a rush of wings and right overhead were the starlings in what appeared as a solid mass of birds making a left turn as I had never seen them do before. They seemed to be almost backpedaling; it was obviously a maneuver done out of fear. Then out of their midst came gliding a Cooper's hawk, with that look of imperial hauteur that only hawks—and some humans—can muster.

To a starling, chasing a slow-winged red-tailed hawk is sport. But when the speedy Cooper's hawk comes along terror strikes their hearts, because the pigeon-sized hawk eats birds smaller than itself—and that includes the starling.

September is the month to see Cooper's hawks as they begin their leisurely migration southward. My guess is that most of the Cooper's hawks we see are this year's young, honing their skills in pursuing prey for the coming winter months.

The preferred food for the Cooper's hawk here on our farm is the mourning dove. The other morning a flock of a dozen doves screamed out of our elm tree and headed for the safety of an evergreen grove, with two Cooper's hawks right on their tails. Again, the hawks must not have been hungry, because they can catch doves on the wing. It was just a practice run. Last winter a Cooper's hawk caught a dove in midair by the corn crib, and after it was finished only a pile of feathers remained. The dove was nearly as big in body size as the hawk.

Some birds of prey—unlike the Cooper's hawk, which will settle for nothing less than freshly killed prey—also feed on carrion. We had a thirty-pound pig that was injured; in spite of our best efforts, Wilbur didn't make it. So I carried him back to the hay field to provide energy for the turkey vultures, which are abundant this time of the year.

Yesterday eight vultures were soaring high in the cerulean sky, silently watching what was going on down below and hungrily eyeing the pig. Then I saw the reason for the buzzards' lofty flight: a bald eagle was soaring lower down and also showing interest in the pig. Soon the eagle, an immature lacking the distinctive white head and tail of our national bird, landed and started to feed. Our daughter Emily got within twenty feet of the majestic bird before it flew, and then only a short distance. When she backtracked, the eagle returned to the carcass.

Today Wilbur is flying high.

SEPTEMBER

To me, autumn arrives with September, even though the equinox won't occur for another three weeks. Already there is a sense of the season seeping from the seams. The leaves of the Virginia creeper are turning to crimson, while goldenrod's yellow adorns roadsides and fencerows; and something about the air is different—maybe because it's spiked with the delicate scent of drying corn and ripening apples.

The waxing moon of the evening will become the harvest full moon by the 9th. Orion dominates the eastern morning sky, and Sirius, the Dog Star, is again visible, faithfully trotting behind the mighty hunter as he follows the Seven Sisters. Sirius is a sign, and a hope, that the ninety-degree days will fade away with August and that now, though the days remain warm, the nights will be cool.

In my opinion, the next eight weeks are the finest of the year. I tend to say the same thing upon the arrival of April, but there is something about autumn as a season that beats out spring. Perhaps it is the leisurely feel of the season; things take on a slower tempo. Even the fall warbler migration dallies along at a snail's pace compared to the spring's rush as the birds hasten to reach their nesting grounds. Common nighthawks seine the evening sky for insects, zigzagging easily, never in a hurry.

During the pleasant warm days of September, young redtailed hawks scream their abrupt cries as flocks of starlings mob them in mock battle. Turkey vultures soar tirelessly for hours contemplating things far below on earth, such as dead chickens, which will fuel those powerful black wings for their journey southward.

Vultures are neat birds: that's why they have naked heads. Otherwise their feathers would become mussed when reaching inside a carcass to grasp a far delicacy. Buzzards are also extremely patient, especially at this time of the year.

To the somber birds, a good meal is worth waiting in line for. One of our neighbor's cows died, and since it was a hot and humid Friday all the knacker guys begged off, so he had to hire someone to bury the cow. But that took time, and as the bloating bovine ripened, an assembly of vultures waited solemnly on the dead limbs of a nearby tree for the right moment.

The other morning a half-grown cottontail was bashed on the road by a car. By dinnertime two vultures were feeding on the carcass. While appearing awkward and clumsy on the ground, the big birds are surprisingly nimble in dodging traffic, waiting until the last moment to open those long wings and flap to safety. It is high in the sky where the vultures become graceful as they ride the rising thermals of heated air.

One of the vultures dining on the cottontail had the dark head of an immature bird. The other one had the red naked head of an adult, likely one of the youngster's parents teaching it the tricks of survival in this fast-paced world.

Turkey vultures prefer to nest on the ground beneath rock ledges and in caves. Locally they often lay their two eggs in hollow stumps and logs or in abandoned buildings. Following an incubation period of about forty days, the young hatch and are fed regurgitated food by their parents.

For a number of years a pair of vultures has nested on the overloft of a barn near Beechvale. The eggs are laid on old leftover hay. After the young are old enough to wander around, they eventually misstep and drop the twelve feet to the barn floor. This first abortive experience of flight doesn't seem to hurt them. When we visited the barn the young were covered with a grayish-white down and were the size of leghorn hens. When we opened the barn door the vultures backed into a far corner and hissed at us in defiance.

Since young vultures don't fly and hunt carrion on their own until they are eighty days old, the immature bird feeding on the road kill must have been newly fledged. Turkey vultures hunt by sight and smell, unlike their kin the black vultures and California condors, which hunt by sight alone. The two on the fresh road kill saw their prey, whereas the great number attracted to the dead cow were lured by, in buzzard parlance, its good aroma.

Ranging from Patagonia to southern Canada, turkey vultures don't have a great fall migration, they just sort of—like some humans—retire southward to food and warmth.

SHREWS

"We don't yet know nearly enough about nature," Alison Deming writes in *Temporary Homelands;* "it truly is an inexhaustible mystery." I get that feeling whenever I see a shrew—and I have been seeing many this fall. Dead ones, that is. The barn cats have been leaving the mysterious little animals on the doorsteps after their nightly prowls. The cats kill shrews and bring them home, but seldom eat them because of their offensive musky odor.

Shrews often are confused with moles, which they resemble. The slate-gray short-tailed shrew, the largest and most common of two species found locally, and the one that our cats are catching, is sometimes called the mole shrew because of the animals' similarities. On close examination, however, there are notable differences. For one, the short-tailed shrew is smaller and slimmer than a mole, and its front feet are like those of a mouse, not like the outward-pointing flipperlike feet of the mole. The shrew's feet are for running, while the mole's are for digging tunnels. A shrew is a racer, the mole a miniature backhoe.

It has been claimed that if the shrew were the size of the lion, humankind never would have gotten beyond the Garden. Because of their high metabolism, shrews have voracious appetites and thus are vicious predators. They consume up to three times their weight, which is one-half ounce, in food every day. If no food is available, a shrew will starve in two days. They are also extremely nervous and can easily die of fright. It's difficult to tame a shrew.

Spending most of their time in subterranean tunnels, usually those created by mice and moles, shrews either hunt or sleep. For a shrew, the pace of life has two settings: high and off.

While primarily a consumer of invertebrates—earthworms, beetles, grasshoppers, snails, slugs, grubs, insect eggs, spiders, sowbugs, and millipedes—a shrew will not hesitate to dine on small vertebrates such as field and white-footed mice. A short-tailed shrew has a unique weapon that enables it to overpower larger prey: its saliva is venomous, containing a poison similar to cobra venom. This is very rare among mammals; the duck-billed platypus of Australia is the only other mammal known to be poisonous.

Unlike a venomous snake, which injects its poison undiluted, the shrew's venom is mixed with its saliva, and only a minute amount finds its way into the wound inflicted by the shrew's razor-sharp red teeth. The venom lowers the blood pressure and causes partial paralysis in the mouse victim.

Since shrews are almost totally carnivorous, their abundance hinges on the amount of prey available. If conditions are favorable, there may be as many as one hundred short-tailed shrews per acre.

One fall a few years ago, some shelled corn in the bottom of our grain bin turned moldy. We loaded the forty or fifty bushels on a gravity wagon and spread it in a narrow band through a field where silage corn had been removed. I forgot about the spoiled corn that fall and winter. The following April when I plowed through that forty-yard strip of now-decomposed corn, I was astonished at the number of earthworms in it and the soil beneath. It was like plowing spaghetti. But what really surprised me was that the plow exposed three grass-lined nests of short-tailed shrews with young. Naturally the shrews were dining on the abundant earthworms. That was the only time I have ever seen the nest and young of the shrew.

Shrews breed from early spring through late fall and have litters of four to eight young. Growing rapidly, the baby shrews are weaned at three weeks; when they leave the nest to learn the skills of the stalk they are fully grown, following their mother through the maze of tunnels in the underworld of the shrew.

When the cats bring home what looks like a young short-tailed shrew, it is probably a least shrew. Even though this tiny shrew, one of the smallest mammals on earth, is fairly common, it is rarely seen. I have encountered only a few least shrews, and those were, of course, dead. Weighing only four grams, or one-seventh of an ounce, the least shrew is one of those mysteries of nature I wish I knew more about.

THE RED FOX

I was unloading manure when I came across the tracks: two sets traveling together, sometimes running straight, then suddenly doubling back to check out a clump of grass. The tracks were doglike and obviously were made by a pair of red foxes out hunting and enjoying the season's first snow. I got down and followed the tracks. At the clump of grass the male had left his calling card, marking his territory. Fox urine has a faintly skunky smell, not unpleasant at all. It is the scent of wildness, and to me is symbolic of the ways of the red fox, a clever, agile, and graceful animal I greatly admire.

I always look forward to the first snow of winter to check out what is living on our farm. Almost every year the first tracks I come across are those of the red fox as he (during the winter it is the male that travels the most) crisscrosses the fields in search of meadow voles. The pair of tracks I followed the other day converged with the tracks of a lone fox coming from the other direction; where they met they performed what looked like a ceremonial dance around two chicken legs.

Earlier in the week our old laying hens had reached the end of their road and became soup and dressing stock. After the gory ordeal of the slaughter I took a wheelbarrow load of remains—heads, legs, skin, and feathers—back to the hay field for the hawks and foxes and any other critters with a taste for chicken. Among the victims was a hen with green legs—one of those special offers from the hatchery, which sounds great at the time but you end up with some weird birds. Anyhow, that pair of foxes found those two green legs, scattered among forty-four pale ones in a jumble of offal, carried them a quarter mile, and played with them. Maybe it was some fertility rite.

Red foxes love to play with their prey. I have seen them catch mice in a hay field and then repeatedly toss the hapless victim into the air and catch it before finally gulping it down. Watching a red fox pursue rodents is watching grace in action. The fox trots along until he pinpoints a mouse; then he stops, cocks his rear legs, and pounces straight into the air. At the peak of the jump he jackknifes and hits the ground and his victim with his front paws—much like a human doing a perfect dive from a springboard.

Red foxes pair off here in January; by March they begin looking for a den site, usually a woodchuck burrow. If the original owner is home, the fox will kill it or chase it out. The fox will then enlarge and clean out the burrow, and in April the three to seven pups are born. For a few weeks the vixen leaves the den only to drink water; her food is brought by her mate. Once the pups open their eyes and begin to eat meat, both parents go out hunting for prey.

Several years ago a pair of red foxes raised a litter in an abandoned woodchuck hole at the end of one of our fields. By the time we were cultivating corn in June the young were leaving the den and playing outside. In time the pups got used to us and we could approach within fifty feet before they would duck into the safety of their home. Around the entrance to the den were the remains of their meals: bits and pieces of fox squirrels, cottontail rabbits, muskrats, and the wings of young red-winged blackbirds. (Of course, there were no traces of the meadow voles: those tender delicacies went down whole, feet, tail, and all.)

To adult red-winged blackbirds, the parent foxes were public enemy numbers one and two. Whenever either of the adult foxes showed itself, a cloud of angry blackbirds would swoop down, flinging all sorts of invective its way. On returning to the den, though, the parents were greeted by the laid-back ears and wagging tails of their pups—appreciative thanks for those young blackbirds.

By September the young foxes were gone. They were now on their own, caught up in what biologists call the fall shuffle, a dispersal that may take the youngster up to fifty miles from its birthplace in search of new hunting grounds and, come January, a mate.

SHORT-EARED OWL

Some of our fields are crisscrossed by sod waterways, grassy strips that filter runoff rainwater during severe storms. Besides preventing soil erosion and keeping the streams clean, the waterways often are home to a variety of wild things. A friend of mine calls them rabbit strips because of the refuge they provide cottontails.

Eastern meadowlarks, red-winged blackbirds, bobolinks, and savannah sparrows nest in the cover as well. Several summers ago a pair of bobwhite quail hatched and raised a family in one of the grass-aster-clover-and-ragweed havens. They stayed until late October when the corn was picked, and then relocated to a nearby overgrown fencerow.

The forepart of this week a sod strip yielded another pleasant surprise. I was shredding corn stalks and was crossing one of the waterways when a crow-sized, tawny-colored bird flushed out of the brown grasses. It was a windy day, and the bird flew (more like blew) downwind mothlike, then circled back and alighted on an electric fence post at the edge of the field. Great! A short-eared owl. I had not seen one of the pretty owls on our farm since the early 1980s, and to say the least, I was thrilled.

Grasping the one-inch-square post top with its taloned feet, the owl was quite tolerant of my presence as I went about my work. It perched there, leaning into the wind and occasionally flicking its tail for balance, until I left for the barn in late afternoon. By that time the owl was ready to begin its hunt for voles and mice in the surrounding fields.

Ohio is at the southern edge of the short-eared owl's North American nesting range. According to existing records, nesting short-eareds in Ohio are rare. Our 1980s sighting had been in mid-July, and that bird may have been one of a nesting pair. Most short-eared owls, however, nest in Canada and Alaska and then move southward to better hunting grounds for the winter.

When the owls find fields that abound with meadow voles, they may stay until deep snow hides their prey. In recent years short-eared owls have congregated in and around reclaimed strip mines, where the grasses, particularly those horrid fescues, are seldom cut out for hay and thus the areas become nurseries for mice and voles—and winter refuges for owls.

The short-eared owl is one of the few owls that begins hunting before dark. Like most predators, owls have their eyes set in the very front of their heads, so they can use binocular vision to see and track their prey. Often short-eared owls can be seen at dusk quartering fields as they hunt for food. Their flight is floppy and irregular and close to the ground, like that of the northern harrier, the short-eared owl's daytime ecological equivalent. By studying the pellets of undigested bones and hair that owls regurgitate, biologists have learned that migrant short-eared owls feed almost solely on small rodents. In one study meadow voles accounted for 75 percent of their diet, with white-footed mice making up the balance.

I would have liked to tell "my" owl to hunt along the east fence line where we have two bluebird houses. There, in grasses and weeds and briars, white-footed mice are numerous. Somehow the white-bellied, bug-eyed little mice manage to shimmy up the one-inch-diameter steel posts and fill the birdhouses with their downy nests of goldenrod seed, where they then settle in for the winter. I wouldn't mind the squatters if they would only, well, go outside when nature calls instead of using one corner of the box. I can understand that sliding down a steel post in zero-degree temperatures may be a bit uncomfortable, but if the mice are left alone the birdhouses literally reek by spring and the bluebirds hesitate to nest in them.

Some ornithologists believe the short-eared owls are declining in number in some parts of their range, and I would have to agree with that assessment. Up until the early 1970s short-eareds visited our farm every fall and stayed through early winter. Then a few years passed before one was sighted. Finally there was a lapse of over ten years. Perhaps the owls are drawn to the vast reclaimed strip mines and simply bypass our farm. I doubt it, though.

Whatever the reason for this particular bird's presence, I am delighted to have the tawny, mice-loving owl of the open spaces back sharing our bit of earth.

WILD COUNT

At year's end I like to take inventory of what's on the farm—
of the wild things, that is. So I travel, walking the woods, fields,
and boundaries, taking note of what's about. Our farm's metes
and bounds mean nothing to the wild animals. They are un-
aware of legal formalities.

In all these seasons—and I've just finished my two hun-
dredth—I've not had a single walk when I didn't find something interesting. After all, there's no bag limit on looking.
The other day, for example, I had a nice surprise at the northeast corner of the farm where there is a rock pile—an accumulation of small granite stones and broken plowshares
picked from the tilled fields over the past 170 years—some
serviceberry shoots, raspberry tangles, and a young hickory.
On my approach a covey of bobwhite quail burst from the
cover and, with wings whirring, flew down the fence line. I
counted eight before they vanished, zigzagging through the
trees, but there could have been a few more.

In the late spring and into summer I heard the clear
whistled call of bobwhites (they whistle their name) from the
fencerow as we worked in the fields. This was the first covey
I've seen this winter, though. I was glad to know that at least
one clutch was successfully hatched and raised.

The northern bobwhite, found throughout the eastern half
of the United States, has declined drastically in number over
the past twenty years. Figures from the National Audubon
Society's annual Christmas bird count show that the bird is
indeed in trouble. In almost 80 percent of the thirty-one states

where the bobwhites are found, populations have dropped sharply. Some states have lost over three-fourths of their quail.

Wildlife biologists aren't sure just why the bobwhites are disappearing from areas where they once were abundant. Of course, there are many theories, and near the top of the list are changes in habitat. Urban and suburban sprawl removes brushy areas, and quail along with it. Weedy fields that once provided nesting places and winter feed and cover are being turned into nicely manicured suburban lawns.

Herbicides and insecticides are also suspected as a cause for the suffering quail population. Many seed-bearing weeds crucial to bobwhites, such as common ragweed, are destroyed by herbicides; this is particularly true in agricultural counties, where the highway department often has a policy of spraying the roadsides with 2,4-D. In those areas the quail get a double whammy, with both the fields and roadsides having a dearth of weed seeds and cover.

Likewise, insecticides—especially those sprayed on hay fields to control alfalfa weevils and potato leafhoppers—kill many of the insects that young bobwhites need during the first weeks of their lives. Not only that, but the bobwhite has a whole slew of predators on its tail. Many nests are destroyed by opossums, raccoons, and skunks, animals that love quail eggs. Should a clutch of eggs avoid detection and hatch after the twenty-one-day incubation period, feral cats and fox will snatch any young bobwhites they find.

The Cooper's hawk is the adult bobwhite's greatest enemy because the swift hawk can easily catch a flying quail. The larger red-tailed hawk is too slow to pose much of a threat to an alert older quail. The covey I flushed was checked out by a local redtail, but the big hawk didn't even attempt to pursue the zooming birds. It must not care for fast food.

In Ohio, the bobwhites were hit hard in the severe winters of 1976–77 and 1977–78. Wildlife officials estimated that some northern counties lost 90 percent of their populations, and in many of those areas the quail simply haven't rebounded to their former levels. Locally, some bobwhites survived those harsh winters, and by the early 1980s their numbers were back up, with the population remaining fairly stable since.

Two years ago I worried about the bobwhites when the Siberian deep freeze hit Ohio and the mercury plunged to minus twenty-five degrees. But even though the bitter cold decimated the Carolina wrens, our quail came through in fine shape. The next spring their cheerful calls again rang from fence posts around the farm. One male serenaded us from the maple tree in the front yard.

As I walk I see the bobwhites' tracks in the powder snow where they feasted on weed seeds and waste corn. I mentally mark my inventory sheet: Bobwhite—doing just fine.

THE WOODS,
CREEK, AND SKY

YOUNG OWLS

This year the great horned owls left their decades-old nest and moved across the road to a smaller, and less desirable, old crow's nest. The crow's nest will suffice for one brood while their old home is being renovated.

I made the discovery of the owl's move while I was cutting firewood late last winter. Having shut off the noisy saw, I was getting ready to load the wood when I heard the crows screaming bloody murder: another skirmish in the endless owl-crow war, and they were headed my way.

I sat motionless and watched the chase. The owl, however, instead of taking off low through the woods, went straight for the crow's nest, landed on it, and settled down on what I presumed to be eggs. Then it saw me. Those wild yellow eyes that had stared with unrestrained hatred at the crows glared at me with like passion. The crows, too, saw me and slunk like black ghosts a short distance away to await the owl's next move. Finally, ever so slightly, I moved, and the owl became unglued and left with the crows in merry pursuit.

I kept checking the nest every week or so but never saw much activity. I did notice that the quality of the small nest— small for great horned owls, that is—was deteriorating. It finally got so bad that the young owls, already nearly the size of their parents, left it and are now half-flying around the woods. Sometimes they are on the ground and sometimes in trees—usually in leaning trees where they can flap and claw their way to the top.

From their lofty perches, the young then beg for food. And

what a variety of fare they are getting. Our woods and bottom pastureland are like an owl supermarket. One evening we walked down to the woods to look for mushrooms when we surprised the owlets. Both flew but gradually lost altitude, like Howard Hughes's *Spruce Goose,* and ended up on the ground. It was obvious what was on the menu for supper: the evening air was rank with the pungent smell of skunk. The young owls, while almost full-winged and having the facial pattern of the adults, were still "hornless" and covered with down. Their talons were razor-sharp, however, ready to grip and slice through hide, or hand, if the opportunity arose. Great horned owls will kill and eat just about anything, especially if two rapidly growing and endlessly hungry young are in the picture. I have found, besides the skunk, the remains of partially eaten rats, cottontail rabbits, and muskrats, and the feathers of robins, mourning doves, mallard hens, and, of course, crows.

At night, incubating crows must present an almost irresistible temptation to hunting owls. They are so open and so vulnerable. And if owls have any memory, it's a grand opportunity to get back at the crows for their pestering habits during the day. If the number of black feathers I find are any indication, the owls have more than evened the score. In fact, I'm surprised any crows survive the nesting season in the neighborhood of an owl family. Crows have a legitimate reason to hate owls, and so the war goes on.

Likewise with mallard hens on their nests. One had a clutch of ten eggs on some old hay bales we are saving for garden mulch. One night last week she disappeared. The ratio of mallard hens to drakes is already around one to four, and the chances for improvement this spring don't look too promising as the owls go about their nightly duck hunts.

It may seem that the great horned owl is merciless to the

small creatures that inhabit our farm. But a duck or crow or cottontail is to an owl what a mosquito is to a swallow, or a cabbage looper to a chipping sparrow, or a fish to a heron: food.

Unfortunately, according to ornithologists the great horned owl will not hesitate to dine on close kin either, which may be the reason the smaller barn owl is disappearing from its former haunts. Barn owls or leghorn—both fill the bill for the great horned owl.

Back to the renovation of the owls' old home: it seems a pair of red-tailed hawks did the work. The hawks enlarged and improved it by adding a six-inch layer of sticks. For payment, the hawks get to use the nest for a season. Last week the female redtail was incubating eggs. If I were a betting man, though, I'd easily wager the farm that by next February the ears of a great horned owl will be protruding above the remodeled nest.

MUSKRAT

Yesterday I surprised a muskrat feeding in the pasture field. It had left the security of the pond and, pushing the wet snow aside with its nose, ventured out almost a hundred feet in search of food. The trail meandered back and forth where the muskrat fed on short pieces of grass. Once it spotted me, the critter dashed for the pond. With the long winter, things must be lean for the humble water rat to throw caution to the wind and provide such a tempting target for the local red-tailed hawk.

On the other hand, if I were a muskrat, I'd take my chances with a clumsy redtail any time over the silent and deadly great horned owl of the night. Redtails often miss their game; owls seldom do. This muskrat survived, even though the dogs picked up its scent and tried to head it off from the spring hole in the ice. The muskrat, however, beat them and disappeared into the frigid water, leaving only a trail of air bubbles to tantalize the confounded dogs.

A muskrat on land is ungainly, but in water it is a creature of grace. Swimming under ice is no problem for the aquatic animal. This muskrat had to swim some sixty feet to reach its den burrowed beneath the roots of the maple tree. There it was safe from predators, if not from hunger.

Last fall I would see the muskrats out on the pond banks, usually early in the evening, gathering mouthfuls of grass and carrying the forage into their den. A few rooms in their maze of underground tunnels were stuffed to the ceiling with the grasses for winter food. Like farmers, muskrats hope to store enough food to last until spring, when they can feast on new grass. If they do run out, as our pond muskrats apparently did, instead of going to the local auction and buying a load of forage, the unfortunate rodents must go hunting for food, and that can be hazardous to their health.

Muskrats thrive in waters and wetlands from the Atlantic to the Pacific and from the Gulf of Mexico to the Arctic Ocean. In the nineteenth century muskrats were introduced into Europe for their luxurious fur. Once established, the animals quickly became pests in the vast canal systems of the Netherlands, France, and northern Germany. The industrious muskrat, with its penchant for digging burrows, almost gave the Lowlands back to the sea.

Ernest Thompson Seton wrote in *Lives of the Game Animals* how the muskrat, according to a legend told by Native Americans, came to settle in its specialized habitat. The god Nanabojou, rewarding the muskrat for its help in the time of the Great Flood, said it could live in any part of the country it chose. The muskrat chose the deep pristine lakes. But the next day the muskrat came back and said it had made a mistake: there was no food in deep waters. So the muskrat chose the grassy banks of the lakes because of their ample food supply. The following day, though, the muskrat again returned, and this time said the banks offered no places to swim. Since the muskrat could not make up its mind, Nanabojou gave it the land in between, neither-land-nor-water, the marshes and swamps. According to the legend, those wetlands are still the muskrat's primary home.

It is in marshes, with lush patches of cattails and other tender green plants interspersed with areas of open water, that muskrats reach their greatest populations.

Since marsh muskrats can't all live in bank dens, they also

117

build houses from vegetation—cattail stalks, spatterdock, sweetflag, along with some sticks. A prime muskrat lodge can be six to eight feet in diameter and rise three feet above the level of the water. As many as a dozen muskrats will live in one large house. Where house muskrats have it over bank dwellers is that parts of their house are edible. In cold weather, instead of diving and digging in the muddy bottoms for cattail roots, the animals can feed on the inside walls of their house.

In the marshes and swamps the muskrat follows close behind the beaver. As the beavers flood new territory, the muskrats soon colonize the fertile, vegetation-rich backwaters. And the Canada goose follows the muskrat. Old rotted-down muskrat lodges provide ideal nesting sites for the geese. While the goose incubates her clutch of four to seven eggs on the top of one muskrat house, the gander will stand guard on a neighboring lodge. Mallards and black ducks also nest on muskrat houses.

CLOUDS

When opportunities drift my way for cloud watching, I usually acquiesce. Sometimes I wonder whether I farm to make a living or whether it is all a front, just an excuse to be out in the fields looking at clouds.

Thoreau thought a cloudless sky is like a meadow without flowers and a sea without sails. I'd have to agree. This week I had several days of great sky and cloud watching. We had six acres to plow for corn, and the weather was ideal: warm enough that rest was needed for the horses and breezy enough that the cumulus clouds crossed the sky like fat sheep trotting across a meadow. When I'd get a crook in my neck from watching I'd plow another round or read Gretel Ehrlich's *The Solace of Open Spaces*, which I carried in my pocket.

We're getting to that time of the year when cloud watching becomes serious, a necessity, almost an obsession—hay making time. When, as a neighbor once put it, we constantly keep one eye on the western horizon.

The first clouds to appear after a high-pressure system has cleansed and cleared the sky are the high-altitude cirrus clouds. True cirrus clouds may be as high as fifty thousand feet and have a thin, wind-swept, wispy appearance. Because they look like the flowing tails of running horses, the lovely, pure white clouds are also called mare's tails. When mare's tails come swishing across the late-spring sky, we hay makers begin to have doubts about mowing the new crop. Rain may be as close as forty-eight hours away.

If the mare's tails are accurate in their forecast and rain is on the way, the next clouds to form are the cirrocumulus. These clouds are thicker and are made of small convection cells that give them the appearance of fish scales—the mackerel sky of weather proverbs. A sky filled with mackerel scales is one of the prettiest of all, particularly early in the morning when the clouds are bathed in the red glow of the rising sun.

Last Sunday morning gave us one of the grandest displays of mackerel scales I've seen in a long time. Actually, the scales were more like the delicate silvery scales of a shiner minnow, small and evenly spread across a wide portion of the sky. In a few places the scales gradually increased in size toward the outer edges until they could justifiably be called mackerel scales.

Following the mackerel scales by a day or two are the heavier wine-dark clouds bearing rain. At this point cloud watching loses its zest.

For me, the most enjoyable clouds to watch are the puffy, low-level cumulus clouds of warm seventy-five-degree afternoons. Sailing like clipper ships through the otherwise clear sky, a cumulus cloud the size of a football field may contain only enough water to fill a bathtub. Even as the clouds race east with the currents of a brisk wind, there is a constant roiling within as parts move into the wind, then turn and billow back into the rest of the cloud.

Cumulus clouds are also an indication of fair weather, those halcyon hay days when heat waves shimmer above the tilled ground and dust devils rise and dance across the fields. The field I was plowing is for some unexplained reason prone to king-sized dust devils. Twice already in years past we had hay raked and were ready to start baling when dust devils appeared and scattered the windrows to smithereens. Clumps of hay were flying as high as three hundred feet; I at first mistook them for soaring vultures, and then, to our chagrin, the hay was dumped into a cornfield. Another day a dust devil whirled down the field and tried to steal my shirt. Whenever I get the chance I run into an approaching dust devil: for a few seconds its whirling wind tears at your clothing and I get a brief cooling off from the summer heat. (Natural air-conditioning.)

Cloud watching can be a tricky business, and I don't see how my tractor-farming friends can do it and not appear indolent to their industrious neighbors. But with animal traction it's as natural as resting horses. We often joke that where tractors can plow a six-acre field in two hours, I figure two days—but my time includes listening to vesper sparrows and meadowlarks and watching clouds scud across the sky.

Recently I was told that great egrets, those lanky white heronlike birds that wade around in murky swamps watching for fish and frogs, are the departed spirits of birders and cloud watchers—which explains that permanent crook in their neck.

TOADS

When I first discovered that the American toad, the common garden dweller, sings, I was dumbfounded. I was maybe ten years old when one April I crept up over the bank of the farm pond to look for the producer of that continuous trilling coming from the water's edge. There, as plain as day, was a warty toad, throat sac puffed almost to the size of a Ping-Pong ball, singing away. And it was a pretty song at that. A toad, that silent critter of summer which spends its evenings and nights snatching up slugs and other garden pests—singing?

This annual spring event had been going on for as long as there had been toads, I just wasn't aware of it. Despite all the rural folklore surrounding the American toad—handling them will cause warts, killing one will turn the cows' milk to blood (this one saved the lives of many toads)—I now knew that toads, at least the males, could sing. And I have been enjoying their spring songs ever since.

Last week when the mercury climbed into the seventies for a day, the toads left the gardens and compost heaps where they overwintered and headed for their favorite ponds. The males, which are smaller than the females, are the first to feel the pull of the ponds. Unfortunately, I saw several that didn't make it; they were flattened on the road. But many survived the hazardous journey and as I write this I can hear them singing, a pure, sustained, musical trill. One of the true and most pleasing sounds of spring.

The spring peepers start piping much earlier than do the toads, and often get frosted into silence. Once the male toads begin serenading the females, however, we know that spring is here to stay and ready to move forward. The toads' steady trill mingles well with the sharper chirps of the peepers and the snorelike calls of the leopard and pickerel frogs.

After the male toads have trilled for a few days, the females begin showing up at the pond edges, where they soon pair off with the finest-voiced males. The mated pair then swims around the shallower parts of the pond, she leaving a double string of eggs, delicate as gelatinous lace, wrapped around submerged branches, weeds, and driftwood.

Once her five to six thousand eggs have been laid and fertilized, the female heads home to the garden or orchard, where she will spend the rest of the year as a dry-land creature. The male, however, continues to trill away, hoping for another mate. After all, if his musical ability attracted one female, it should be good enough to impress others. So he and others of his kind send their sweet voices out twenty-four hours a day——unless extreme cold drives them to silence.

If the weather remains warm the toad eggs begin hatching within a week. Soon the bottom of the pond is covered with tiny black tadpoles looking like strewn commas. Of the thousands of one pair's progeny, fewer than a hundred will survive to leave the waters of their birth. If the tadpoles venture too close to shore where there is no cover, great blue and green herons, grackles, crows, and ducks will be waiting for them. Should the tadpoles turn to deeper water for safety, they become fish food. Life for a tadpole is along a razor-thin edge.

By midsummer the toad tadpoles will have developed lungs, grown four legs, and absorbed their tails for nourishment. One by one they now leave the pond and head cross-county. In September I have seen young toads no bigger around than a quarter in the middle of fields plowed for wheat. The little toads must be finding food there, and life is probably safer in a field than in the pond where thousands of their brothers and sisters disappeared down the throats of predators.

Female toads don't mate until their fourth spring, when they are lured to water, often to the pond of their birth, by the songs of the males. Male toads may return a year or two earlier. By their efforts and skills as musicians, our springs are richer.

MORELS

This morning I strung some fence and turned the cows into new pasture. It was drizzling, and since I carry all my fencing material in an old trapper's backpack, I had the flexibility to take the long way home—the path through morel mushroom country. And they were there, but not where I had anticipated finding the tasty fungi.

Instead of around recently dead elm trees, the mushrooms I found today were in the open pasture fields where there once were apple trees. Those trees have been gone for decades; not even a trace remains to be seen. I only faintly remember a few rotting stumps, and yet these long-dead descendants of Johnny Appleseed's generosity are still producing a crop—of mushrooms, that is.

In the vicinity where I found the morels, one apple tree is still alive, or rather one branch of it. Standing on the cellar wall of a now-gone farmhouse, I visualized where I would plant apple trees if I were a settler. I traced an imaginary line along the curving bank to the living tree at its far end. Then I walked the bank and filled my coat pocket with morels.

My friend Bob Mohr from Winesburg, who collects and grows antique apple varieties, has a clone of this remnant apple tree growing in his orchard. Once this tree succumbs to old age, its tissue will continue to live and bear fruit on a young tree. Bob named it the "Calmoutier" apple, in honor of the community that originally planted and nurtured the tree. These French settlers elevated the growing of apples to an art.

The morels I found were what local mushroom hunters call

the gray morel or sponge "mushruin," the earliest one to appear. I like cloudy, drizzly days for morel hunting, especially in pasture fields, because the mushrooms stand out like beacons against the green background. Since the cool weather has kept back the grasses, the morels were almost as tall as the grass and easy to spot. I could see them without my glasses.

This spring, interestingly, the morels are appearing in areas where they were common ten or even twenty years ago but have been absent in recent years. One place in our pasture field where we find a few every year, however, produced forty-four gray morels this week. If that is any indicator of abundance, this may well be a banner year for spring mushrooms. And the best is yet to come, with the appearance of the larger yellow morels in the next few days.

Around dead elm trees is still considered to be the best place to find the yellow morels. I know some morel enthusiasts who look nowhere else. And when that one tree is found, nothing else matters for a while.

Last year I came across one of those trees in a heavily hunted woods. It was well hidden in a thicket of multiflora roses, and when I got down on hands and knees to check it out I almost couldn't believe my eyes. Spread around in a five-foot radius from the trunk of the dead elm were over twenty six-to-seven-inch-tall yellow morels—all at their peak of perfection, fresh honeycomb tops with that rich earthy aroma.

This part of the country has two commonly occurring native species of elm: the American or white elm (*Ulmus americana*) and the slippery or red elm (*Ulmus fulva*). Both are susceptible to Dutch elm disease, and both are dying in large numbers. Once the elms have died and their bark is peeling off, conditions are "right" for mushrooms. At this stage it is also difficult to tell the two species apart, though the slippery elm may have a more reddish wood where the bark is stripped away.

I have come to the conclusion, after a number of years of in-the-woods "research," that the dead American elm is the true host of morel mushrooms. The slippery elm seldom has any growing under it. But I keep checking all dead elms; after all, I may be wrong, and finding that one tree with morels is worth the effort.

Actually, hunting for morels isn't any effort at all. In fact, it is a sensation of deep pleasure simply to slip away for an hour or two to be among the great variety of wild living things: the flowers—trillium, saxifrage, phlox, and ragwort; the flowering trees; the birds—migrating warblers, singing vireos and tanagers and wood thrushes, gobbling wild turkeys; and even the soon-to-be-gone woodland fungi. What more could one desire?

LIFE ON THE EDGE

"For both farmer and monk," writes Kathleen Norris in *Dakota: A Spiritual Geography*, "time is defined not by human agency but by the natural rhythms of day and night, and of the seasons." Yesterday was the summer solstice, the time when the sun reaches its northernmost point and "stands still" for a short time before beginning its six-month journey to the south and the winter solstice.

Now, officially, it's summer: the season of heat and humidity, growth and ripeness, when time slows and life reaches its greatest abundance. The first day of summer was a good representation of what the season can be—sultry, oppressive heat. Work-stopping weather, too hot for man or beast to labor. So we went swimming.

A farm pond in ninety-degree weather is pure bliss, and I soon noticed that life around the edge of the pond was flourishing in the high temperatures. There was a flurry of activity as damselflies and dragonflies zipped and zoomed from overhanging grasses and weeds to driftwood surrounded by green algae. For them the heat was great.

While the others cooled off in the clear water of the pond's center, I floated on a half-deflated and still-leaking inner tube along the edge. I wanted a frog's-eye view of what was going on in the shallows.

The slender and delicately pretty damselflies, some blue, some pale green, some reddish, were everywhere. Grasping the female by the neck, the male damselfly assisted her in finding suitable spots to deposit her eggs. They would fly in tandem, like twin helicopters in perfect synchrony, and then suddenly drop to alight on a blade of grass hanging into the water. If there was room, the male would land too; if not, he would hover as she laid her eggs on the underside of the grass blade. Then off again to a new location. Once when I slowly raised my hand to the water's surface it seemed to suit the male damselfly, and the female deposited an egg on the side of my partially submerged finger. Now I am party to the fecundity of a June pond.

When damselflies are at rest they hold their similarly shaped fore and hind wings vertically over their bodies. The bigger and stouter dragonflies rest with their wings outstretched. With their four powerful wings, dragonflies are fast fliers, having been clocked at sixty miles per hour. Since adult dragonflies catch their prey, which includes gnats and mosquitoes, on the wing, speed is important to them.

Adult dragonflies are wary insects. Resting with their bulging compound eyes always on alert, they take wing as soon as danger threatens. Taking advantage of their speed and endurance, dragonflies range far from water. Last week I saw several different species hawking over the hay field at least half a mile from the nearest pond or creek.

As I continued my journey through the algae along the edge of the pond, creatures would brush against my legs. Once a startled bull frog exploded out of the water from under my face. Then it was my turn to be startled. All along the edge I found, on weed stalks and pieces of driftwood, the empty skins of dragon- and damselfly nymphs, or naiads (their larval stage), where they had crawled out of the water, split their skins, and emerged as fully developed, air-breathing, flying insects. The skins looked like pale ghosts guarding the pond.

Once the dragonfly or damselfly eggs hatch, the naiads live

underwater and may go through ten to fifteen molts before emerging as adults. The naiads are voracious feeders, consuming large numbers of mosquito larvae and other aquatic insects. They may even prey on newly hatched fish. The naiads of the largest species of dragonflies, such as the common green darner, may reach two inches in length before they climb out of the water and, as adults, hawk and hunt like true predators.

Worldwide there are 5,000 species of damselflies and dragonflies; 450 of those are found in North America. Around our pond there were, at most, a dozen species. But that was enough to make it interesting.

The green darner's scientific name is *Anax junius,* which means Lord of June. Back in my boyhood creek-exploring days, we simply classified dragonflies as fliers, and all were lumped under the order of "snake doctors." Damselflies, to us, were "flitters," darting from weed to weed. We didn't know that the green darner was the Lord of June.

WATCHING

Rarer yet than a cold day in June is a morning in early August when the temperature is in the mid-forties. We have had several of those crisp mornings now, and they have been pure bliss.

The weather front that brought the cool Canadian air also cleared away the haze, and Orion, along with the Dog Star and the Seven Sisters, were visible in the crystalline eastern sky before daybreak—a preview of autumn.

I managed to find time on one of those mornings to sneak off to the woods. At the time we fenced our woods off from the livestock twelve years ago, we also built a wooden platform twenty feet up in the crotch of a red oak near the eastern edge of the woods.

The platform was initially intended as a stand from which we would collect our year's supply of venison. Our aspirations have failed to materialize. The only blood drawn as a result of our carpentry has been from scratches and scrapes climbing up and down the tree.

Anyway, this particular morning I climb up the crude steps (which seem to be growing farther apart) and settle onto the planks, several books by my side, feet over the edge, back against the tree. Catching my breath, I wait—for what I don't know. The air grows chillier. I am tempted to put my coat back on, but no, I want to revel in this reprieve from the summer's heat.

There are farm sounds: a rooster crows, heifers bawl; I hear the senseless gabble of a pair of barnyard geese, the noise of a milk truck. From the woods a pewee calls, a squirrel barks, a woodpecker hammers, a cardinal sings, cicadas whine, a leaf drops, and across openings to the sky chimney swifts speed.

The swifts must be migrating, as there are dozens of them just above the trees searching for any insect that might stray from the safety of the foliage.

Then in front of me, what looks like a down feather drops, but too slowly for a feather, and it drops by jerks, four to five inches at a time. Once it reaches eye level I see that it is a tussock moth caterpillar, quite common at this time of the year. Less than an inch long, the bristly-haired white caterpillar is dropping and hanging on at the same time, releasing a single strand of silk, a lifeline in case of misjudgment.

Lowering itself several more feet, the caterpillar stops and appears to have doubts about the whole deal. With an eastern towhee scratching in the leaf litter below and a black-billed cuckoo calling from a nearby tree, life is certainly perilous for the little white worm. Its hopes of being blown to another tree and a change of diet are dashed when the breeze dies down and it hangs motionless at the end of the silken thread.

It changes its mind. Slowly it begins inching its way up the lifeline, as if rewinding it. Like a young athlete on a chinning bar, up and down, a quarter-inch at a time, up it goes.

I start to read an essay by Barry Lopez on how he and two friends returned to the scene of the Bear River Massacre in Idaho to plant a potted sulphur buckwheat in remembrance of the unnecessary deed. In 1863 the Second Cavalry decided to "chastise" the Northern Shoshone Indians; they did so at Bear River by killing over three hundred Shoshone, a hundred of whom were women and children. On the corner of the map Lopez used to find the location someone had written, "Not a Sparrow Falls. . . ."

As I finish reading, the caterpillar has reached the tip of the oak leaf where it had attached the thread and plunged into the unknown. Now it climbs back onto the leaf. Safe at last.

Obligations beckon; I get up and stretch my legs. A young red-tailed hawk, riding the thermals created by the warming sun, screams its short, immature cry. A gray catbird meows in protest. And I think, "Not a sparrow shall fall without your Father's consent."

RED SQUIRREL

After an absence of at least thirty years, red squirrels are back in our woods: five of the spunky little squirrels were seen last week. It is common for animals in the mixed coniferous and deciduous forests of the northern United States and Canada to go through population cycles. The ruffed grouse, red squirrel, and snowshoe hare all reach peak numbers every eight to ten years, and then for some reason their population plummets. When the numbers of snowshoes hares, for instance, are high, the populations of their predators, such as the lynx, marten, fisher, and fox, also increase. When the hares hit the low point of their cycle, predators that depend on them also decline.

This far south, population cycles aren't as evident, or may be absent altogether. I often wondered what happened to the little red squirrel after they disappeared from this neighborhood sometime in the early 1960s. Did disease wipe them out, or was the decline part of a long-term population fluctuation? In any event, although a thirty-year cycle sounds a bit long, they are now back and as feisty as ever.

The red squirrel brims with energy and shares with the blue jay the duties of sentinel of the woods. While it is less than half the size of its cousin the fox squirrel, it is twice as loud. The red squirrel's shrill scold lets all other denizens of the woods know that there's danger afoot. Be it hunter, fox, or house cat, the word is out: every creature has been duly warned.

In fall and winter the red squirrel—or pine squirrel, often

shortened to piney—sports a rusty red coat across its head, back, and tail, is olive-gray along its sides, and has a grayish-white belly. To top off the handsome coloring, its ears have tufts of dusky hairs, which make it distinctly different from the fox and gray squirrels in appearance. It is easy to tell the red squirrel from its larger kin—for most people, anyway.

Locally there's an old story of a big-city hunter out for his first squirrel hunt, all decked out in new clothes, stopping at a farm and asking permission to hunt squirrels. "Sure," the farmer said, "just don't shoot my cows." Within an hour the hunter was back at the farmstead with his limit of four, three grays and a fox—or so he thought. When the farmer saw that the hunter had three chipmunks and a piney, he didn't have the heart to tell him different.

Years ago hunters thought of red squirrels as vermin, in the same class with rats and starlings, since they competed with the more desirable fox squirrels for food and denning places. It was also commonly believed that the red squirrel would harass and sometimes neuter the male fox squirrel. An outdoor magazine once published a series of photographs of a red squirrel supposedly caught in the act of performing the ghastly deed—though the quality of the pictures made the one of the Loch Ness monster seem crystal clear. For a long time, in any event, red squirrels were indiscriminately shot on account of their bad reputation.

Adding to the red squirrel's ill repute was its taste for birds' eggs and nestlings. For that reason birds hate the piney almost as much as they do the screech owl. Birds' eggs are only a seasonal delicacy, however. For the rest of the year the little red eats what other squirrels do, which includes a wide range of nuts, acorns, conifer seeds, berries, and tree buds.

Young red squirrels are born in May and June, usually four

or five to a litter. Born blind and helpless, their eyes open after four weeks, and at the end of six weeks the young are weaned. The mother squirrel keeps her family together throughout the summer, training them in the ways of gathering food. Here in September, when five or six are seen in one tree eating beech nuts, they are likely a family. The male red squirrel isn't with the family; he's off somewhere else in the woods making mischief, or looking for it.

When the red squirrels disappeared from our farm back in the 1960s, the fox squirrel population increased dramatically, and their numbers stayed up. They enjoyed a long peak cycle. It will be interesting to see whether their numbers will decrease now that the red squirrels are back competing with them for favorable habitat. Several fox squirrels did move into our yard this summer. Perhaps it was to get away from the noisy newcomers.

It could also be that the red squirrels are returning for but a brief sojourn, since they are known for their population fluctuations. Even if it is for just a short while, it is nice to have them back after thirty years.

NUTS

I am sitting here listening to Hurricane Opal fling chestnuts off the roof. There is a chestnut tree at each end of the log building, and the fury of the wind-driven rain is dislodging the nuts from their protective burrs—*clunk*—then rolling them over the edge. Last evening we picked up two gallons of chestnuts, and now there are at least that many down again.

Right now is the season of wild edible nuts. Besides chestnuts there are black walnuts, hickory nuts, butternuts, and hazelnuts, all free for the picking. And you don't even need to own the tree. No pruning, no spraying: all you have to do is harvest the crop. There are many more delicious wild nuts being produced than are used—even though the squirrels and chipmunks do their best to cache as many as possible for winter food.

The easiest tree to spot right now is the black walnut, because they drop their leaves early, while the green tennis-ball-sized nuts are still on the tree. Walnuts are also the most difficult to prepare for storage, since the nut is covered by a thick, moist hull.

The mushy hull has to be removed before the nut can be dried and stored. There is no easy way to do the messy job. Some walnut lovers place the nuts on their driveway and let the tires do the hulling. Others grind them underfoot until the hull is removed. We use one of those old hand-cranked corn shellers; it works superbly.

An absolute must for working with fresh black walnuts is a pair of rubber gloves—unless one wants purple-stained hands for a very long time. Once the walnuts are hulled, the nuts are washed and then spread out to dry in the sun. After a week or more in the October sun the nuts can then be placed in cotton bags, or wire or wicker baskets, and placed in a cool, dry spot. If correctly prepared, the nuts can be stored uncracked for several years, and they still retain their freshness.

I think black walnuts are at their finest au naturel, simply cracked and eaten. They have a rich and robust flavor. Of course, they can be used instead of pecans or English walnuts in pies, cakes, and nut breads. Their rich flavor carries through, though it is maybe a bit too "walnutty" to suit some tastes.

Milder and less of a hassle to preserve are the hickory nuts, both shellbark and shagbark. Both trees grow straight and tall and have long strips of gray bark that curl at each end. While the hickory nut is also encased in a protective, four-part hull, it separates naturally from the nut. The nut can then be gathered ready to be dried and stored.

There is great variation in the quality of hickory nuts. Although both the shellbark and shagbark nuts are sweet, the shellbarks tend to be bigger and the meats easier to pick when cracked. Rarely, a hickory is found that produces nuts which roll out in halves when the shell is cracked. Our neighbors are lucky enough to have one of those on their farm. Hickory-nut cake is a well-known autumn delicacy in many parts of rural America.

Butternuts aren't as common as the walnuts and hickories, and it is hard to get the meats out in large pieces, unless the nuts are soaked in hot water for half an hour and then allowed to cool before cracking. But the delicately flavored nut meats are worth the effort. Butternut pie is one of nature's finest desserts, comparable to wild blueberry pie.

Hazelnuts are the American version of Europe's filbert, a

138

small nut the size of a marble. Hazelnuts in the wild usually grow as shrubs along fencerows. The nut is covered by a thick, hard shell, but its meat is as crisp and sweet as the cultivated filbert.

The chestnuts that are bounding off the roof are not native to these parts: they are Chinese chestnuts, which are resistant to the blight that devastated the stately and abundant American chestnuts in the early part of this century. The old-timers who remember the days of the native chestnuts claim that these orientals are only a fair substitute for the smaller but sweeter nuts of the American chestnut. I don't know; I have never tasted an American chestnut.

The chestnuts can be roasted, but they also make fine eating after being stored in a heated room until the nut meat begins to dry away from the shell. That's when they attain their sweetest flavor. Their's is a smell and taste as rich as October.

FALL MUSHROOMS

It is said that there are young bold mushroom eaters, but no old bold mushroom eaters. The careless ones eventually come across the beautiful but deadly destroying angel (*Amanita virosa*)—which has some similarities to the common and edible meadow mushroom—fry it, and eat it. The amanita can kill its consumer within twelve hours.

Most of the poisonous mushrooms appear in late summer and fall, and that is when I become cautious in collecting edible fungi for the table. There are, however, a few delicious fall varieties that I feel comfortable gathering, and one of those is the sulfur shelf (*Laetiporus sulphureus*). Another name for this delicacy is chicken mushroom, because when it is sliced and fried in butter it tastes like the breast of chicken.

I had been keeping my eyes open for a sulfur shelf all fall without success. (Unlike the springtime morels, one sulfur shelf goes a long way.) They grow on decaying logs and stumps and usually are found from July through October. Last spring I found, on a rotting blown-down tree, several sulfur shelves from the previous fall—or rather, the shriveled winter-killed remains of the prized mushroom. I kept checking the old log, but no new mushrooms sprouted.

Then the other morning my luck changed. I was passing an old ash stump in our pasture field when I spotted, growing from near its base, a nice clump of fresh chicken mushroom— bright orange above and a rich sulfur yellow below. I broke it off from the stump, tucked it under my arm (it was as big as a football), took the horses' lead rope, and headed for home with my coveted possession. I was as happy as a Frenchman with a fresh Périgord truffle.

That evening we had fried strips of chicken mushroom, along with sliced sweet peppers, tomatoes, onions, and several kinds of cheeses, on bread—a sandwich that made the Whopper look like a wimp.

The sulfur shelf also makes a deluxe omelet. Sliced bits of the tender mushroom are sautéed in butter, to which we add small amounts of green pepper and onion and then the scrambled eggs. Salted to taste, the omelet makes breakfast an event. What's so nice about finding a fresh sulfur shelf is there is enough mushroom to last awhile. Which allows the chef to wax creative.

Another fall mushroom we have the courage to eat is the giant puffball (*Calvatia gigantea*). As with the sulfur shelf, the puffball has to be fresh to be edible. That means that when sliced its flesh must be pure white; if it isn't, the mushroom is too old for eating.

Many of us are familiar with the ripe puffball: when we step on it a cloud or puff of greenish-brown smoke bellows away. When I was young the local lore was that if the smoke of a puffball got in your eyes you would be permanently blinded. But that didn't keep us from stomping on the ripe puffers: we just made sure we faced into the wind. Nevertheless, when I ate my first puffball I was hesitant at first to get that close to something with the reputed ability to blind.

For anyone interested in sampling wild fungi, especially fall mushrooms, a good field guide like *The Audubon Society field Guide to North American Mushrooms* is a must. Better yet, accompany someone who can identify the mushrooms, both edible and poisonous. Some species are only mildly poisonous, causing intestinal upset.

141

I have come across the deadly amanita, or destroying angel, only a few times. It is one of the prettiest of our wild mushrooms: pure white with a delicate cap and gills, and a ring, or annulus, partway down its graceful stem. It is said to also be the most delicious of mushrooms. I wouldn't know. I prefer the chicken mushroom: it may not be the tastiest of fungi, but at least you live to talk about it.

SCRATCHING THE WOODCHUCK

The origin of the term "Indian summer" is somewhat clouded. Even the time when it should make its appearance tends to be debated. But when Indian summer does arrive, we recognize it and know that it is a wonderful time of the year. One point of common agreement is that it comes only after several killing frosts have ended the growing season. Or better yet, after a spell of wintery weather ("squaw winter"), for then we can enjoy the short season of warmth and sunshine all the more.

The term "Indian summer" is thought to have originated in the northeastern United States. It first appeared in American literature in 1778 when John Crèvecoeur, a farmer in New York's Mohawk Valley, mentioned it in his *Letters from an American Farmer* when relating his experiences with American Indians. Apparently the Indians made use of the summerlike weather during the waning weeks of autumn to stock up for the coming winter months.

Indian summer occurs when a high-pressure weather system moves southeast across the Great Lakes to the Atlantic coast, where it becomes stationary. The high pressure holds all approaching weather fronts at bay while allowing some warm southerly air to reach the Great Lakes and the Northeast.

Actually, these same weather patterns can occur throughout the spring and summer. Often called a "Bermuda high," the system then produces daytime temperatures in the nineties, along with high humidity. We had a week of it in late August this past summer, when we sweltered in the heat and motionless air while filling silos. The difference between an August Bermuda high and Indian summer is that the latter has temperatures about twenty degrees cooler, and we enjoy every minute of it. The pleasant spell may last for only two days or as long as a week. It may even occur several times in an autumn or, rarely, not at all.

My guess is that few people, with the possible exception of country schoolteachers and poets, love Indian summer more than we farmers do. It is a time when we can catch up on the work that was pushed off during the busy season. Often, though, Indian summer comes late enough that most of the preparations for winter have already been made: gardens have been put to bed for the winter, the silo is full, hay mows are still filled up (though, in this drought year, not as high as we would like to see them), the woodpile is ready to meet the onslaught of winter, and the last apples have been squeezed into cider.

Besides the little odd jobs, there is time for walking; and Indian summer is one of the finest times of the year to read the messages of nature. Following the closed-in feeling of summer, when our vistas are blocked by corn and other field crops, we again live in open country. Seeing the harvested and brown cornfields evokes in my memory the lines from Whittier's "The Corn Song":

> *Heap high the farmer's wintery hoard!*
> *Heap high the golden corn!*
> *No richer gift has Autumn poured*
> *From out her lavish horn!*

In a sense, Indian summer is a summary of the seasons. The warm breeze has the softness of spring; the soil still holds the warmth of the summer sun; the woods, although the hardwoods are mainly bare of leaves, are afire, the ground ankle deep with the colors of autumn; and the air already has the clarity of winter.

Animals, too, enjoy the short warm spell. One Indian summer day as I was walking in the woods, I saw a woodchuck napping in the sunlight at the base of a tree. Since the woodchuck had its home in the woods, it got very little of the sunshine that its cousins out in the hay field did. Now, with the leaves gone from the trees, the overweight animal could get full benefit of the warm sun. Walking silently, I eased up behind the tree to take a closer look at the snoozing woodchuck. With its bulging sides, it looked like a loaf of homemade whole wheat bread. Taking my walking stick, I reached out and lightly scratched its back. Instead of waking, as I expected it to, the woodchuck arched its back in appreciation; its movements seemed to say: "Ah, that feels good. Now over here. There, there. Mmmm . . . that's good." Quickly I backed away, leaving the woodchuck to its dreams and to the Indian summer sun.

Birds are also busy on Indian summer days. Yellow-rumped warblers feed on the remaining white berries of the gray dogwoods, while robins feast on the red fruit of the flowering dogwoods. As the robins, which have changed from a tame dooryard bird to a wary woods bird, jostle for the berries, they drop almost as many as they eat.

Red-tailed hawks soar lazily on thermals of warm air—until, that is, a late-migrating flock of blackbirds finds them and gang-attacks one. The hawk circles and gains altitude. At the great height the tightly grouped blackbirds almost disappear as, in perfect unison, they turn one way, then immediately flash the other way—like the opening and closing of a venetian blind. It all seems a game as the pursuit of the black-

145

birds and the evasion of the hawk continue in the clear sky, until finally the attackers tire of it and turn to look for another redtail.

A few late asters are still in bloom, their lavender and blue petals and orange centers adding color to the season. Goldenrods are already shriveled and brown, and have been for some time because they bloomed so early this year; a few were showing yellow florets in late June. The fluffy dried flowers-gone-to-seed are drifting away on the wind. Milkweeds, likewise, are emptying their boat-shaped pods and sending a new generation through the autumn air. Although the growing season has ended, new beginnings are already astir.

WRENS

One morning last fall I was walking down the pasture field to get the horses when suddenly a loud, lively bird song—"TEA-kettle, TEA-kettle, TEA-kettle"—rang from a multiflora rose-bush near the creek. My first thought was, "That cardinal sure feels good." As the song was repeated time and again it dawned on me that it was not a cardinal signing, but a Carolina wren.

I have a slight disability when it comes to birding: I can't hear bird songs in the higher frequencies. Thus I have difficulty hearing some species of warblers, and the four-note song of the Carolina chickadee is two-noted to me. However, I have no problem hearing the Carolina wren. Maybe that is why I enjoy its song so much.

The Carolina wren is common in the South, hence its name. During mild winters it steadily extends its range northward, only to retreat in harsh winters. In the 1960s and early 1970s the wren was a regular nester in this part of the country. For several summers a pair raised their young in nests built in empty cans and odd corners of our shop. Then came the severe winters of 1976–77 and 1977–78. The bitter cold and the blizzard of January 1977 took a heavy toll on the able songsters, and the even worse blizzard a year later finished the job. Ornithologists estimated that 90 percent of the Carolina wrens in Ohio died in those two years. The bird I heard singing was only the second one on our farm since those rough winters.

One ingenious pair of wrens survived the first cold winter handily. Our neighbor Ervin Weaver, who operated a general repair and buggy business, had a pair of wrens nest in his shop in the summer of 1976. Besides repairing about anything that came down the road, Ervin stocked a full line of farm-related hardware. If we farmers had need for plowshares, mower parts, v-belts, shovel handles, gloves, or whatever, he usually had it. Since the roof leaked a little right above the glove display, he draped a piece of clear plastic over a part of the rack to divert the rainwater. It was there beneath the plastic that the wrens built their bulky nest. Since few gloves are sold in the summertime, the wren pair successfully fledged five young.

In the fall the young wrens left to seek territories of their own. But the adult pair stayed around, oftentimes inside the shop, which they entered through a small hole in the east wall. When the blizzard arrived that January morning, and the temperature dropped by noon from thirty degrees to five below, the wrens were snug and safe inside Ervin's shop, warmed thoroughly by his Hitzer stove.

The following year the wrens weren't so fortunate. Because the weather was mild for several days preceding the storm, they were roosting outside when the front edge of the blizzard hit before morning, and the little wrens perished.

With the mild winters of the late 1980s, the wrens are trekking northward again and our local population is slowly recovering.

The Carolina wren is the largest of the five species of wrens around here. It is rusty brown above and buff below, with a white chin and a conspicuous long white stripe over the eye. Its near look-alike, the Bewick's wren of the southwestern United States and the Pacific coast, was once fairly common in Ohio. Their numbers peaked around 1950, but then, for reasons not fully understood, the Bewick's began a dramatic decline, to the point where today it is rarely seen. Some blame its disappearance on competition from the feisty house wren.

Almost everyone is familiar with the house wren, a gifted songster that is a favorite of many people. House wrens are aptly named because they often nest near houses and seem to like being around humans. Bluebirders, though, aren't too fond of the little wrens, since they have a habit of hogging nesting boxes put out for bluebirds. It wouldn't be too bad if a pair of wrens would nest in one box and be satisfied; but usually the hyperactive male stuffs all the neighboring birdhouses with sticks, thus preventing other birds from nesting.

House wrens also have the nasty habit of destroying other birds' eggs. Last summer a pair of bluebirds had just begun their second nesting in a box on the edge of our truck patch, several hundred feet north of our house, when a pair of house wrens moved into an empty bluebird box south of the house. Since the two pairs were so far apart, I thought the wrens wouldn't cause trouble for the bluebirds. But a few days later I spotted a wren in the north garden, and when I checked the bluebirds' nest, the eggs were already punctured. Needless to say, I was upset.

Likewise, several years ago we were fixing fence along the woods when we flushed a female cardinal from her nest in a thorn apple tree. The cardinal had barely left the tree when a house wren darted in and promptly pecked a hole in one of the eggs. Why the wren did the mischief was hard for me to understand. Surely the cardinal wouldn't be competing with the wren for nesting sites. As one writer said, "The house wren is of irritable disposition"; perhaps that's the best explanation there is.

Unlike the Carolina wrens, which are year-round residents, the house wrens migrate south for the winter and don't re-turn until late April or early May. Even with their "irritable dispositions," the house wrens are nice to have around, though. What other bird can sing while holding a worm in its bill? I've noticed, too, that the dispositions vary greatly among pairs. We had one pair nesting by the house that never bothered another bird. Whereas the next pair to come along may be as ornery as only house wrens can be.

One wren we see only in the wintertime is, naturally enough, the winter wren; it is tiny (the smallest of the wren tribe and the only wren native to Europe, where it is simply called "the wren") and has a stubby tail. We usually see only one or two of the reclusive birds annually, almost always in the tangled tops of fallen trees or about the roots of trees along overhanging creek banks. One we saw last winter was very cooperative; it flew to a fallen American elm, and we got within fifteen feet of the little migrant as it searched, almost mouselike, for food in the moss and crevices of the decaying tree.

We have been told that the winter wren sings an indescribably beautiful song in its nesting grounds. Friends of ours, Bob and Caroline Mohr of Winesburg, traveled to the Great Smoky Mountains, and near Gatlinburg, Tennessee, at a place called the Chimneys, they heard the wild and beautiful song of the winter wren. Although there have been a few reports of winter wrens nesting in Ohio's hemlock ravines, their usual nesting grounds are in the boreal forests of Canada and down the crest of the Appalachians.

Our other two wrens are birds of the wetlands. The marsh wren nests in cattail marshes. Its football-sized nest is woven to the stems of cattails about a foot above the water. Marsh wrens are much more often heard singing their loud, gurgling song that ends in a chatter, than they are seen. Sometimes the male flies above the cattails and sings while fluttering back into the marsh. My best looks at marsh wrens, save for one occasion, have been mere glimpses. During the nesting season marsh wrens sing day and night.

Nesting on the grassy edges of wetlands, in wet prairies, and in sedge meadows is the sedge wren. Ohio is on the eastern edge of the sedge wren's range, and in recent decades its local numbers have declined. It is now rarely seen away from the Lake Erie marshes. I have only once seen this wren of the sedges. Its song has been described as a chattering trill, resembling the rattling of a bag of marbles.

Wrens, with their eruptive energy, are unique and interesting birds. One writer, in Bent's *Life Histories*, described the Carolina wren like this: "The nervous little creature appeared to be full of a sort of compressed air, which escapes from time to time in a series of mild explosions, like the lid of a teakettle being jarred up and down by steam."

I have hopes for the Carolina wren's return as a nesting resident. This winter one kept me company while I cut firewood from a downed beech tree (possibly the same one I heard sing in the fall). The energetic bird scurried through the thicket of branches and explored every knothole along the trunk of the tree. Every so often it would scold, saying what sounded like "ker-r-ring" or "te-r-r-rp." And then it would sing its wonderful song, which had the magical power of stopping my splitting maul in mid-swing.

NORTHERN LIGHTS

On a clear, cold, starlit evening in early November 1991 a new dimension was added to my appreciation of the natural world. Soon after sunset there were signs in the sky that something special was in the making. Reddish beams of light appeared from the northwestern horizon, reaching to a point almost straight overhead. As the evening progressed, more lights appeared, and it was evident that a great show of the aurora borealis was occurring.

Red lights from the west were joined by red hues from the east, while to the northeast and lower down, curtains of green, blue, and white shimmered across the night sky. After maybe thirty minutes the aurora began to fade, until only patches of red remained. But shortly afterward the colors returned even more vividly as reds from west and east converged in an apex above.

Covering the apex were gauzelike sheets of white, almost like a fiery mountain with a snowstorm crossing its peak. To the north and northeast drapes of white and green unfurled as if someone were shaking out a carpet in slow motion. The lights would diminish, only to spring back to life again. For almost half an hour we stood with upturned faces—spellbound by the beautiful spectacle. Only rarely, maybe once in a lifetime, does such a brilliant display appear as far south as Ohio.

Since I had read somewhere that the Eskimos claim the aurora makes crackling and whistling noises, or sometimes flapping sounds like a flag blowing in a storm, we listened. We heard nothing. The Eskimos also think that if one whistles

152

softly, the lights will draw nearer. I tried it and was promptly told by one of the children to please be quiet. I understood; it was as if I had desecrated hallowed ground—like whistling in church. The aurora was so bright, so vast, and so new to us that it evoked feelings of awe and reverence.

Almost all the polar explorers in the 1800s and the early part of this century expressed similar feelings when in the presence of an aurora. Edward Ellis, a nineteenth-century adventurer, wrote: "I pity the man who says 'There is no God' or who can look unmoved to the very depths of his soul by such displays of infinite power."

Charles F. Hall, another polar explorer of the 1800s, exclaimed: "Who but God can conceive such infinite scenes of glory? Who but God could execute them, painting the heavens in such gorgeous display?" And the British antarctic explorer Robert Falcon Scott wrote: "It is impossible to witness such a beautiful phenomenon without a sense of awe." (In the southern hemisphere, where Scott explored, the lights are called aurora australis or southern lights.)

Besides mentioning a spiritual presence when writing about the aurora, many explorers expressed the inadequacy of words to describe something so strange and beautiful. A Royal Navy officer wrote about the northern lights in the 1850s, saying: "No pen or pencil can portray its fickle hues, its radiance, and its grandeur." Likewise, an expedition to the arctic in the 1880s prompted Adolphus W. Greely to write: "The aurora of January 21st was wonderful beyond description, and I have no words in which to convey any adequate idea of the beauty and splendor of the scene."

The northern lights have fascinated humankind since ancient times. While philosophers and scientists from Aristotle to Ben Franklin puzzled over and sought a logical explanation for the apparition, the common folk created legends. In the southerly latitudes of the northern hemisphere, where the northern lights are seldom seen, and where vibrant red is often the predominant color when they are, a bright aurora was an omen for disaster. To the people of Europe, likewise, it suggested battles and blood. When a red aurora occurred over a wide region of the northern hemisphere in the early 1940s, the Russians took it as a sign that they would finally triumph—after a long and bloody struggle—over the Germans. Locally during this same aurora, a farmer and his wife were out in their field setting up corn shocks when the northern lights appeared in the night sky. Alarmed, the farmer said to his wife: "The end of the world is at hand; let's go to the house. We won't be needing this corn."

Unlike the people in the lower latitudes, the Eskimos consider the northern lights a friend, not a foe. This is probably because they see the aurora so frequently—one night out of three from October through March. In the past, some Eskimos believed that the whistling and crackling sounds which sometimes accompany the aurora were the footsteps of departed souls tramping about on the snows of heaven, or that the lights were torches held by the dead to help the living hunt during the dark of winter.

Other once-held beliefs concerning the cause of the northern lights were that they were lost lightning from the earth or the explosions resulting when warm and cold air meet. Scientists have known for over seventy years that the northern lights are not caused by reflected sunlight. They did, however, discover that the sun plays a role in another way. Scientists predicted that 1990, 1991, and 1992 would have brilliant shows of northern lights, because these were peak years of intense sunspot activity. Indeed, it is during such peaks in the eleven-year solar cycle that the northern lights are most likely to be visible at lower latitudes.

The northern lights are created by a series of events I do not pretend to comprehend and even scientists do not fully understand. In times of high sunspot activity, intense flares of electrically charged particles erupt from the sun and generate a strong solar wind. As the solar wind nears the earth, it meets the earth's magnetic field. This invisible shield around the earth blocks most of the solar wind; however, if the discharge from the sun is powerful enough, some of the charged particles (protons and electrons) become trapped above the atmosphere in a donut-shaped area around the geomagnetic poles. (These poles lie about eight hundred miles away from the geographic, or true, North and South Poles. In the northern hemisphere, the geomagnetic pole is near Thule, Greenland.)

As the charged particles enter the donut-shaped ring, they speed up, and some shoot into the earth's atmosphere. The energy released during this process creates the northern lights. If the particles strike oxygen atoms, the glow may be red or yellow-green. Should the particles collide with nitrogen atoms, blue and bluish-white lights will fill the sky. Naturally, a combination of atoms colliding at different altitudes may result in an aurora with varied colors.

A deep red aurora like the one we saw in November was probably the result of oxygen atoms being charged at extremely high altitudes. The top of the curtains may have been 250 miles high, while the bottom edge of an auroral curtain is usually some 75 miles above the earth. The curtains may extend for hundreds of miles horizontally. The converging pattern of the aurora we saw, which came to a point slightly south of straight overhead, is called a corona.

155

An hour after the aurora began to fade I went outside again. The starlit night showed not a trace of northern lights. The charged particles generated from the sun were spent—or so I thought. At eleven o'clock they were back: not as a corona, but flitting and dancing across the northern sky. A final showing.

TUNDRA SWANS

Sometime in mid-November I begin to listen for the final proof that winter is about to arrive. (As if I need final proof with the temperature at twelve degrees Fahrenheit this morning!) Several times we thought we heard it, but it turned out to be the far-off barking of a beagle in hot pursuit of a cottontail rabbit. Any day now, though, it will be the real thing: the high-pitched calls of migrating tundra swans.

Regardless of what we're doing, we always have time to stop and watch the swans. Against the blue sky of the clear and cold late-fall day, the whiteness of the swans stands out, and it is easy to distinguish them from migrating geese. Their wingbeats seem slow, but they are powerful, and soon the swans are out of sight.

The tundra swan used to be known as the whistling swan until the American Ornithological Union decided, sometime in the early 1980s, to change the name. At the time it bothered me; but now, in hindsight, I think the AOU was correct in their choice. The call of the swan does not at all resemble whistling. And since the swans nest in the arctic tundra, the new name is very appropriate.

In late winter and early spring, when the regal birds leave the broad waters of Chesapeake Bay in Virginia and the bays of North Carolina and begin their long flight northwestward to their nesting grounds, they are often forced to wait out cold weather. Sometimes thousands of tundra swans rest and feed on Lake Erie awaiting more favorable conditions to continue their journey. Occasionally, in years when Lake Erie is completely frozen over, the only open water the swans can find is the Niagara River above the falls. Then at night, while the swans sleep with their heads tucked under their wings, they float downriver and are swept over the falls. Many are killed or too injured to fly.

During the spring migration the swans often stop inland, away from Lake Erie. It is not unusual to see a flock of thirty or forty swans in our local swamps along the Killbuck or in the backwaters of the Black Fork Dam. Since swans eat water plants—as much as fifteen pounds of wet vegetation a day—the swamps are ideal for the hungry migrants.

Tundra swans, like other swans, mate for life. When the pair reach their summer home—a territory that extends from Southamptom Island in northern Hudson Bay westward to Victoria Island, and on along the northern and western coasts of Alaska—they stake out their nesting territory. A couple will usually claim one square mile for their own and use the same area all their lives.

The swans prefer to nest on small islands in shallow tundra pools. Using mosses and grasses, the swans build a bulky nest three feet across at its base and from a foot to two feet above the water. The finished nest resembles a muskrat house.

In the moss-lined depression on top of the mound, the female swan, or pen, will lay four to five creamy-white eggs. If the pen has enough body fat, she will fast for the five-week incubation period. While the pen broods the eggs, the male, or cob, stands guard, much like a male Canada goose. In case the pen must leave the nest to feed, she carefully covers the eggs with moss and down to protect them from parasitic jaegers and other bird predators that love to dine on eggs.

Soon after the young swans, called cygnets, hatch in late June or early July, the parents lead them to a larger body of water, where the adults molt and are unable to fly for six to eight weeks. The cygnets grow rapidly feeding on the abundant aquatic life in the long daylight hours of the short arctic summer. By the time the adults have grown back their flight feathers, the young are almost ready to join them in flights across the tundra.

As summer turns into autumn and ice begins creeping along the edges of the arctic pools and lakes, the swans are in no hurry to leave. They linger and continue feeding on the nutrient-rich vegetation, which is converted into much-needed fat. The fat is fuel for their long flight south.

Finally, sometime in October, the smaller lakes become ice-bound and great flocks of swans begin flying southward. The cygnets, now fully grown, look grayish-brown next to the snow-white adults.

Partway along in their journey the huge flocks split. About half of the population of tundra swans veers to the southwest across the Rockies, to winter in the great inland valleys of California. The other half of the population flies southeast and may cross our Ohio farm on the way to the bays of the Atlantic coast. Unless the swans are forced down by bad weather, inland stops during the fall migration—unlike during the spring flight—are uncommon. Some do stop on Lake Erie for food and rest.

If the cold advances slowly, the tundra swans may fly south over a period of several weeks, usually between November 8 and 20. But should a sudden and furious arctic storm arise, thousands of the migrating swans may pass over in a single day. If the big birds have the benefit of a brisk northwest wind, they may move along at well over sixty miles an hour.

In years past it was only after the swans left their nesting grounds that they faced their greatest threat: humans. During the peak of the fur trade, the Hudson's Bay Company also dealt in swan skins. From 1853 to 1877 they sold 17,671 swan skins, which were in demand for the millinery trade as well as for their high-quality quills for writing and drawing.

As a game bird, the tundra swan never saw much demand. Although young birds were apparently edible, the old birds were said to be too tough to eat. This is understandable, since swans live to be fifteen to twenty years old.

Even though the swans were not choice eating, their large size, striking white plumage, and graceful flight made them tempting targets for gunners. When the swans finally were given full protection under the Migratory Bird Treaty Act in 1918, their numbers began to increase. Even today, though, in states where swan hunting is illegal, some are shot by hunters claiming they mistook the swan for a snow goose. They must be stretching the truth quite a bit, since it would take a lot of imagination to mistake a stocky, relatively small snow goose for a swan. And besides, a snow goose has black wing tips.

A few states may still allow tundra swan hunting—I know Utah does—but in most regions of North America the "swan song" is no longer heard. Although that legend is often passed off as mere fancy, there are those who believe it is true. Merrill Gilfillan, for example, writes in *Moods of the Ohio Moons* of a Columbus, Ohio, man who shot a swan: "When he shot, the swan, fatally wounded, set its wings and glided to a distant landing where it collapsed. It was calling constantly as it glided, a chilling, plaintive series of notes of great beauty. The man, a hardened hunter, was deeply moved by the experience." He had heard the song of the dying swan.

Last fall a lone tundra swan stopped at our pond for a day. It even flew with the geese to the cornfield. In the midst of the geese the white swan appeared twice their size. Ever alert, it stood with its long neck outstretched as we watched from the barn. There was something sad about the lone swan. Maybe it was the absence of other swans. Then we noticed that the noble bird was limping. After the geese had finished feeding and took off for the pond, the swan followed. Hobbling along, its powerful seven-foot wingspread stroking the air, the majestic bird at last became airborne. Its limp having vanished, the swan became a bird of grace.

Sometime that night, the lone swan left. Maybe it heard the soft, almost musical calls of its migrating kin in the cold, thin air and joined them on the final leg of their long flight to the Atlantic coast. I wish the lame swan well.

WOODMAN, SPARE THAT TREE

Now that December is here and the winter solstice only three weeks away, when the days will be short and the nights long and cold, we spend a lot of time cutting firewood. All the trees we cut are dead. Elms dead from Dutch elm disease, ironwoods and ashes dead from the competition of the taller trees, an oak that took years to die.

Ridding a woodlot of dead and diseased trees seems the logical and right thing to do: it establishes order in the forest. But as I lay the saw to the base of a dead elm, a voice whispers in protest: "Woodman, spare that tree." It is my inner voice, my conscience, speaking for the creatures of the woods that depend on dead trees for survival.

Of the resident songbirds wintering here in our woods, over half spend the cold nights in the cozy cavities of dead or dying trees. This includes the chickadees, nuthatches, tufted titmice, Carolina wrens, bluebirds, and all the woodpeckers. A dozen or more bluebirds may huddle together in one cavity for extra warmth and comfort during frigid weather.

Besides the songbirds, owls such as the great horned, screech, and the rare saw-whet, and the American kestrel, our colorful robin-sized falcon, also use tree cavities for winter roosting. Likewise, most of the mammals of the woodlot live in tree dens. While the raccoons and the red, fox, and flying squirrels primarily use standing den trees, opossums, skunks, gray foxes, weasels, and cottontail rabbits prefer hollow logs for hiding and denning places.

Dead trees and snags are as much a part of a healthy natural woods as growing trees. For that reason we are careful about which dead trees we cut. Ironwood, a tough tree that thrived when our woods were grazed (until twelve years ago), is simply too hard to be of any benefit to cavity-living animals. A woodpecker would need a drill and chisel to create a home in a recently dead ironwood. It makes superb firewood, though. Among the finest. So does the slippery (red) elm—again, a wood too hard for birds to work. Excellent firewood; it equals ironwood.

Woodpeckers are cavity builders, and most prefer the softer trees like the American (white) elm, red maple, and aspen. Every spring the woodpeckers excavate new holes for their nests (the flicker will reuse old cavities), leaving the previous years' cavities for other species of birds. Nationwide, eighty-five species of birds nest in cavities formed in dead trees. Sixteen of those species have nested in our woods, from the wood duck to the Carolina chickadee.

Dead and dying trees also provide an abundance of winter food for birds. Soon after a tree dies, bark beetles (of the family Scolytidae) arrive, lay eggs, and when the larvae hatch they eat tunnels across the wood beneath the bark. After the larvae pupate, transform into adult beetles, and fly off in search of new host trees, the tunnels remain as engravings on the dead tree's surface.

The female bark beetle lays her eggs along the sides of an oblong nuptial chamber; as the larvae emerge, they begin eating their way outward. This creates interesting and beautiful patterns, especially on American elms. Today when we were cutting firewood I peeled away the loosening bark of an elm and admired the artwork of the beetles—beetle hieroglyphics. Some patterns resembled large spiders, while others looked like sunbursts. A few had their outleading tunnels so close together that they looked like flying butterflies.

163

Bark beetles winter over in all stages—as adults, pupae, and larvae. And the birds know it. Woodpeckers, in particular, feast on the beetles in the wintertime. Where there are dead elms one can always find a downy woodpecker probing for bark beetles. Chickadees also get their fair share of the energy-rich delicacies.

Dead trees in a woodlot are far from lifeless as they return to humus. We leave most of them for the wild things, and warm our feet by the heat from the tight-grained, rock-hard, woodpecker-resistant ironwood and red elm, spiced with a dash of oak, hickory, and cherry.

THE COMMUNITY

CHRISTMAS HOLLOW

It wasn't until the early 1970s that I "discovered" Christmas Hollow. Our church services were held on the farm where the hollow is located. One Sunday on an impulse, before leaving for home in the early afternoon, I decided to check a clump of evergreens for winter birds.

The trees were about a thousand feet northwest of the barn, and upon reaching the evergreens, which proved to be hemlocks, I was astounded to find that they were on the rim of a sheer drop-off of eighty feet or so, with a creek at the foot. For a few minutes I stood and absorbed the wild beauty of the scene. Then, following a cow path that descended over a hogback to the bottom of the hollow, I entered a dense stand of hemlocks, some up to three feet across. And there were the birds.

It was around Christmastime, and although several inches of new snow lay on the ground, beneath the canopy of hemlocks there was only a dusting of snow. A band of chickadees and a golden-crowned kinglet were busy in the protected cover. As I approached, the small birds disappeared, only to instantly reappear when I softly imitated the call of a screech owl. The chickadees scolded "seet, seet" as they almost alighted on my hat, while the kinglet stayed in the background. Then, what to my wandering eyes should appear but a red-breasted nuthatch, working its way headfirst down the trunk of a hemlock tree.

Of course, I couldn't stay in this idyllic place for long, since I had told my wife I was going out to hitch up the horse when I got the sudden notion to explore the hollow. We have, however, returned many times since to that place of pristine beauty.

What sets Christmas Hollow apart from our other woodlands is the hemlocks. It is not often that such thick stands of the pretty trees are found in this part of the country. Where the Doughty Creek flows through Troyer's Hollow is one area where the evergreens flourish, and there are a few other pockets, but none is as near to our home as Christmas Hollow.

The Canada (or eastern) hemlock (*Tsuga canadensis*) is native to the Great Lakes states, the eastern United States, and southeastern Canada. Hemlocks are shade-loving trees and so naturally thrive on north-facing bluffs like Christmas Hollow. When mature, they reach a height of sixty to seventy feet and a diameter of two to four feet.

What saved many of these hemlocks, besides the ruggedness of the terrain, was the inferior quality of their wood. It is light, soft, and brittle. When it is used at all, it is for coarse lumber and pulp wood. Another disadvantage of sawing hemlock logs is that when the lower branches die, sap collects where they were attached to the trunk and, in time, knots of pitch are formed. These knots are glass hard and can chip and dull saw teeth. Sawyers don't like hemlock logs.

In the 1800s many hemlock trees were cut for their bark, which was rich in tannin, an oil used in tanning leather. Today, tannin has been replaced with synthetic agents and the hemlock bark is no longer needed.

Even though the hemlocks may not be in great demand for lumber, they are excellent trees for wildlife. Besides the cover they provide, deer, ruffed grouse, and rabbits will eat the buds and the filmy sprays of tender needles. Many birds feed on the seeds within the three-quarter-inch-long cones, which grow on the ends of the twigs. White-winged and red crossbills, especially, are fond of the light-brown seeds, which they find by prying apart the scales of the cones with their unique bills.

During the severe winters of the late 1970s we found pine siskins and the colorful evening grosbeak feeding in the crowns of the hemlocks. The hardy birds seemed at home in the trees, which must have reminded them of their summer homes in the coniferous forests of Canada and New England. Since then we haven't found any of these irregular winter visitors in the hollow. Of course, that isn't to say they weren't there when we weren't.

Many other birds make the hollow their home or visit while migrating. My wife and I paid a visit to the spectacular gorge this past May. It was toward the end of the spring warbler migration, and a good number of the little birds were still around. Some were obviously lingering migrants, but others may well have been planning to nest in the hollow.

Perhaps the highlight of that day was a pair of Louisiana waterthrushes, members of the warbler family. We surprised one of them as it was taking a bath in the shallows of the shale-bottomed creek. As we worked our way up the hollow the warbler stayed ahead of us. Sometimes it ran across the flat stones along the creek's edge, pausing occasionally and bobbing its tail like a spotted sandpiper. All of a sudden it took flight, alighting on a hemlock branch that drooped low over a pool formed by a fallen tree, and then it sang its song: clear, high, and rapid. A wild and rollicking song that fit well with the seclusion of the place and the murmuring of the water as it cascaded over the fallen tree. My guess is that the waterthrushes were a resident pair, since they are known to nest in the darker ravines of eastern Ohio.

The wildness of the hollow isn't restricted to hemlocks and

birds. Here, on a knoll above the rim of the gorge, the rare trailing arbutus thrives, blooming with delicate pink blossoms in early spring. And I'm sure, if more time could be spent exploring the entire forty-five-acre hollow (not all of which is hemlock covered), other rare wild plants could be found. Possibly the small shade-loving mountain maple, which often grows in the midst of hemlocks. Its leaves look like those of the common red maple; however, its twigs are a dark olive green.

Christmas Hollow wasn't always a quiet and secluded place. In the 1930s two men, Maurice Herald and John Crosby, leased the coal rights for ninety-nine years from the owner of the farm. The two then opened a mine about thirty-five feet down from the top on the steepest part of the bluff. Using an ingenious Model T Ford-powered windlass, they winched the coal cars to the rim, where the coal was then sold and loaded onto trucks and wagons. For around six years the hollow (called Dry Run Hollow back then) bustled with activity. Sometime in 1937, owing to the depression and the thinning of the coal vein, which made digging difficult, the mine was closed. For a number of years the mine entrance was still open to anyone with a spelunking spirit.

Sometime in the past decade the entrance caved in; all that remains now is a woodchuck hole into the mine, which is used by, besides the woodchuck and its kin, raccoons, opossums, skunks, and foxes, living in comfort in their own underground Holiday Inn. The mine is cool in summer and warm in winter. The temperature stays in the mid-fifties year round.

The only visible signs today of the mining endeavor are several room-sized depressions in the pasture field above the mine, where portions of the excavation caved in. Nature has reclaimed the hollow for its own.

PEEPER BOG

Last night I made my annual pilgrimage to Peeper Bog to listen to the frogs'—spring peeper and wood frog—proclama-
tion of the arrival of spring. I, and the frogs, couldn't have
chosen a better evening. It was one of those rare times when
everything turns out right.

There was so much to see and hear and smell and feel that
my senses were racing each other feeding bits of information
to my brain. A naturalist once said, "Look for the little things."
But wait: first my eyes had to take in the big picture.

To the east there was a total lunar eclipse, and the bottom
edge of the full moon was just beginning to brighten, like
molten gold in a crystal fish bowl, when I reached the bog.
Earth was rolling through space at a thousand miles a minute
to get out of the way so the moon could regain its shine.

Further on, in the western sky, brilliant Venus was in con-
junction with the Seven Sisters. Only rarely does Venus meet
up with the Pleiades. The constellation is shaped like a little
dipper, and Venus was just off the end of the handle.

To the northwest, a bit closer to Venus than to the North
Star, the fuzzball Comet Hyakutake was speeding on its way
away from earth. Standing there by the bog and watching the
sky I thought of the words of John Muir: "When we try to
pick out anything by itself, we find it hitched to everything
else in the universe." While my eyes beheld the beauty of the
night sky, my face was touched by the pleasant breeze bearing Gulf of Mexico heat, warmth that softened and dried the
earth and set the plowmen and frogs off. At the same time, I

smelled the rich aroma of nearby freshly turned soil and the faint scent of a distant perturbed skunk.

But the sounds: the sounds of those lustily singing frogs are the voice of spring. April music. A declaration from the tiny amphibians that even though the winter was cold and long, they made it, and this forty-degree water feels just fine.

To me, the shrill chorus of a bog full of spring peepers and wood frogs is one of the finest sounds in nature. The peepers, unless disturbed, will call incessantly—night after night, week after week—so long as the weather stays warm. The low-key clucking of the wood frogs, on the other hand, must take much more effort, because they croaked and carried on like a flock of ducks for about ten minutes and then abruptly lapsed into silence. For at least ten minutes there was not a single cluck from their section of the bog.

Were the masked frogs resting for their next session, or had the brightening moon spooked them? But then one started calling, followed by two more, and eventually the whole gang was at it again. The hilarity of it all even triggered a screech owl into adding its quavering song from one of the pin oaks along the bog edge.

The wood frog doesn't worry about the return of cold and ice. It ranges farther north, beyond the Arctic Circle, than any other North American frog and is used to being frosted into silence. Unlike the peepers and most other frogs, the males of which are the first to arrive in the vernal pools, wood frogs arrive at the mating waters at the same time. Thus the little frogs get a leg up on the first warm spell of spring: within a matter of days they mate, lay their three thousand or so eggs, leave the water, and head back to their summer haunts in moist woodlands.

When I left Peeper Bog the wood frogs were in their rest mode, but the peepers were going full tilt. The moon was only a dimple away from being back to fully bright. Venus was sinking toward the western horizon, and the North Star, reassuringly, was still in the same place.

COLTSFOOT

Perhaps it is because of the long winter of waiting for spring that we cherish the season's first flowers so much. The crocuses and snowdrops in the gardens and flowerbeds have been in bloom for a week or more already. Now the first wildflowers are showing their colors as well: the dandelion-like coltsfoot that blooms in profusion in the full sunlight of sheltered road-sides and ditch banks.

Unlike the later-blooming dandelion, coltsfoot bursts into blossom before it sends up any leaves. Its yellow daisylike flowers are on short, scaly, greenish stems that push through the winter's accumulation of leaves and litter to brighten the waysides—a refreshing counterbalance to the empty Pepsi and Bud Light cans and discarded Marlboro cartons.

Coltsfoot is an alien and a relative newcomer to this part of the country, having arrived only in the past several decades. The early New England colonists planted it in their gardens for use in herbal medicine, preparing a decoction of its flowers and leaves as a cough remedy. The hardy plant eventually es-caped the confines of the garden and turned wild.

Since coltsfoot, again like the dandelion, disperses by air-borne tufts of downy seeds, it would seem the little flower faced almost impossible odds spreading west into the prevail-ing winds. But west it came, though it took several centuries to reach this part of Ohio.

With real estate developers doing their utmost to fill in and pave over many pristine parts of the community, one would think a tiny newcomer like the coltsfoot would find it tough to gain a toehold. Remarkably, it found its niche in an especially harsh environment—in the gravel along roadways.

Right now with the cold and rain and the season in ebb, the coltsfoot has folded its blossoms and waits for the sun and warmth to return before it again splashes the roadsides with yellow. It is only after its flowers fade and turn to winged seeds that the leaves appear. These have the shape and size of a yearling Percheron colt's foot, hence the flower's delightful name.

Now that spring is in momentary retreat, we have more time to enjoy this special time of the year. As Henry David Thoreau put it, "Live in each season as it passes; breathe the air, drink the drink, taste the fruit, and resign yourself to the influences of each."

I always feel cheated when, near the end of April or early May, a massive high-pressure system moves off the coast of the southeastern United States and forgets to leave, thus opening the door to warm Gulf air currents and summer arrives overnight. The birds that chase the spring northward then pass us by in their haste to reach their nesting grounds; the woodland flowers, which often bloom for several weeks as our coltsfoot is now doing, then burst into flower, set seed, and wither within a week. And of course, the farm fieldwork goes ahead at full throttle. That must be why I feel cheated: the busyness doesn't allow me time to walk in the woods.

We need time to savor the special things in life: to take a child's hand in our own and share in the child's wonder at the unfolding of a leaf—the blue of a robin's egg, a bee on the yellow blossom of coltsfoot. Pliny the Elder regarded coltsfoot as the best herb for lung complaints. For those of us weary of winter, it's also good for the heart.

WILDFLOWERS AND PLACES

After sitting on plows and planters, harrows and discs, for many hours of the spring, and now with the last of the seed corn securely in the soil, I was ready for a walk. A long walk. So yesterday I set out for points west. The place I had in mind embraces some of the most rugged and unspoiled beauty in this part of the county: Christmas Hollow. The gorge is home to the Louisiana waterthrush and the yellow-throated warbler, which I hoped to see. But mainly I went to botanize—to see wildflowers and ferns.

After getting permission from the farm's owner, I walked downstream. Wildflowers abounded and birdsong sifted through the hemlocks in the sheltered hollow. This spring has been made to order for us nature snoopers. The cool weather has extended the wildflower, mushroom, and migrant bird seasons for at least a week. And here on the steep north-facing slopes the wildflowers were almost two weeks behind those on flat land or on slopes exposed to the sun. Many of the ferns were still curled in fiddleheads.

Although what seemed like acres of white trilliums were over their peak of beauty and beginning to show traces of pink on their white petals, other wildflowers were in their climax bloom. Wild geraniums and phlox with their showy lavenders, along with white baneberry and dainty rue anemones waving on slender stalks, sparkled on the slopes. Here, too, I found the tallest and handsomest jack-in-the-pulpit I've come across in many years: nearly three feet off the ground, Jack looked smug in his rich purple-and-green striped pulpit.

Scattered in among the wildflowers were the ferns, a nice

mixture of Christmas, wood, and New York. I saw only a few of what I consider to be the prettiest of the family, the maidenhair fern. With its black stems and delicate fronds, the maidenhair is a real treasure.

The nicest discovery came when I began climbing out of the hollow and found a clump of hepatica. Of course its flowers, which bloom in mid-April, were long gone. But the leaves by themselves were beautiful. Three-lobed and dark green, they reminded me of African violets. What was surprising was that these were the sharp-lobed hepatica instead of the round-lobed variety I was acquainted with. A new one for me.

I looked around. There were hepaticas everywhere! Up the slope and across as far as I could see. Using the binoculars I spotted even more.

I sat down on a log and pondered what this place must have looked like back during that warm week in April when the hepaticas were in full bloom. Not only that, but it struck me how much I'd been missing all these years I didn't know about Christmas Hollow. To think that this secluded garden was within walking distance, albeit a long walk, of the country school I attended when our naturalist-schoolteacher would bemoan the fact that there were no hepaticas to be found.

The hepatica is considered by many to be one of our loveliest wildflowers. Blooming early in the spring on the end of hairy stems that push up through winter-weathered leaves, the flowers range from pale lavender to rich purple. The white ends of the stamens shining against the deep blue-and-purple cup have been said to look like stars on a summer night.

I didn't see the waterthrush or yellow-throated warbler, but I hope to return next spring to see the steep slopes resplendent with hepaticas.

177

Last May I found a steep wooded slope in Christmas Hollow covered with hepaticas. At that time the pretty flowers were long gone and the clumps of three-lobed leaves, which grow after the plant has flowered, were everywhere. My desire was to return this spring to see them in bloom. Yesterday I did, and what a treat it was.

The hillside was now covered with delicate and beautiful flowers, ranging from pure white and pale pink to lavender and (my favorite) sky blue, to almost purple. The inch-across flowers appear on the end of hairy four-to-five-inch stalks, and each clump may have up to a dozen stalks and flowers. Their beauty is unrivaled this early in the season.

Their earliness is one of the reasons I cherish the hepaticas so much: they dare to bloom when most of the spring's wildflowers are only beginning to show signs of life, the trees are still winter bare, and even the ferns haven't begun to unfurl their fiddleheads. Their blossoms are already gone by the time the migrant birds arrive. The scarlet tanagers and vireos and rose-breasted grosbeaks never see hepatica flowers.

I had the good fortune to be in the company of some Wilderness Center botanizers when I went looking for the hepaticas. On our way down into the ravine we found several low-growing trailing arbutuses, their aromatic flowers not out yet. Here and there a few spring beauties defied the cold to show their flowers.

We saw two bloodroots in bloom, their waxy white flowers showy in the afternoon sun. Cut-leaf toothwort and blue cress were in bud waiting for more sun and warmth before they burst into bloom in a week or so. The trilliums were only just pushing through the winter-worn leaves and had six to eight inches of growth to go before blooming. They will be the common wildflower a month from now.

The trillium's day is yet to come; now everything belongs to the hepatica. The common name for hepatica is liverleaf or liverwort, which hardly anyone uses. The ones we saw were the sharp-lobed hepatica (*Hepatica acutiloba*). Its thick leaves live through the winter and have turned to a deep maroon-and-green by the time the flowers appear in early April.

Even now, while the hepatica is in full bloom and splendor, new leaves are beginning to sprout. By mid-May the flowers will have been replaced by a lush growth of new and lovely three-lobed leaves. The old leaves will die back, to become part of the rich humus nourishing the plant. Those lush clumps of new-growth hepaticas were what caught my attention last May.

Last year I was by myself when I found the hepaticas, and since it was after the middle of May, the trees were in leaf, the woods were ringing with bird song, and the flowers were white trilliums, rue anemones, downy phlox, and jack-in-the-pulpits. Everything about the place—its seclusion, its life, its beauty—had the aura of hallowed ground. As a friend calls these special wild places, it was a small honey spot. The wind in the trees and the water flowing over the shale-bottomed creek seemed to whisper, "Do not come closer. Take off your gumboots, because you are standing on holy ground." So I did.

Our return this spring, and the sight of the hepaticas in bloom, reaffirmed my belief that many of us need wild, unspoiled places where we feel close to God. Places that are becoming scarcer and scarcer in this part of the country. Fortunately, the owner of this tract of land appreciates the treasure he has. For years he has paid taxes on this forty-five-acre "wasteland," with very little monetary return. What counts is that he preserved it and kept it unspoiled. For that we thank him. Now many benefit from his generosity and foresight.

179

As Aldo Leopold wrote, "There are some who can live without wild things, and some who cannot." I am one of those who would have a hard time doing without wild things, and places. In so stating, I think I speak for all of those botanizers, aged ten to eighty, who walked down that hollow to look at the lovely hepaticas in the renewal and rebirth of spring.

FALLOUT

If you expect the worst, you're never disappointed. But occasionally there is a day when everything turns out right, or even better than your highest hopes. Three friends and I had such a day last week.

All through April and the forepart of May the weather was cool with the winds out of the north and northwest—conditions less than ideal for the northward flight of migrating birds. Of course, there was a steady trickle of them: the bobolinks and swallows and Baltimore orioles arrived right on schedule. But there was no great flight.

During the night of May 9 the wind shifted, blowing now from the south, and a pent-up river of birds broke and began moving north. Then it rained on the 10th and through the morning of the 11th, forcing many of the migrants down again in northern Ohio. The result was what birders call a "fallout" of migrating songbirds, especially warblers.

It was fortuitous that the 11th had already been circled on the calendar a month or more ago as the day the four of us would get together and spend a leisure day birding the local area.

Bill Mohr from Berlin and I had been invited to join two top-notch birders for the day. Bill and I did considerable birding together twenty years ago when we puttered across the state in a goldfinch-yellow VW Beetle. Neither of us was ever a serious lister, though. We never got caught up in the blitz of chasing down rare birds. Sure, we'd keep track of birds we saw—daily and annual lists, maybe. And I've kept a record of birds seen on or over our farm, which, with the cerulean warbler added last week, now stands at 173 species. But I have no idea what my life list of birds would be.

We started out at 4:30 in the morning so we could do some "owling" in the Killbuck Marsh Wildlife Area. By playing a recording of owl talk, one can entice owls to come close. A barred owl checked us out from a branch fifteen feet above us. We also tried to call in rails, shy birds that skulk through marshes. A sora and Virginia rail answered, their voices heard over the pickerel frogs' snoring and the spring peepers' yelps of "Too deep, too deep," but didn't show themselves.

Since it was raining, we decided to travel north along the Killbuck to Overton for a coffee break, checking en route for shorebirds around the mud flats of the numerous ponds and lakes in the pretty valley.

In the windless lee of the trees along the road we soon saw that we were in for a rare day. Warblers, vireos, orioles, and tanagers by the score were working the treetops for insects. Just north of the village a Swainson's thrush sang, a new song for all of us. South of town we found a golden-winged warbler and a wealth of other warbler species.

When we backtracked to the wildlife area we saw a bald eagle, heard sandhill cranes, and continued to rack up warblers. At two o'clock we left for Mohican State Forest, where we hoped to see nesting warblers that seldom show up farther north.

We soon saw the prairie and hooded warblers. East of the covered bridge, along the Clearfork, one of our guides imitated the call of the screech owl (he sounded more like an owl than a real one does). His quavering call seemed to cause all the warblers on the opposite hillside to abandon their resistance to gravity, and a wealth of birds drifted down to the river's edge. Among them were the Canada and worm-eating warblers—new ones for the day.

West of the covered bridge we saw the yellow-throated warbler and the Louisiana waterthrush, also a warbler. On the ridge the pine warbler and purple finch were singing. And then came what was the highlight of the day for me: the singing of the hermit thrush. Mohican is one of the few places in Ohio where this secretive bird of the north woods and mountains nests, and sings. Now, though, three thrushes were singing at the same time, one fairly close by—a beautiful, clear, flutelike song. I wrote along the margin of my field guide next to the hermit thrush: "Heard it sing, 5/11/95 at Mohican; heart-intoxicating sweetness—wild, lovely, other-worldly."

Just before dark we arrived at the home of one of our "guides." His nine-year-old son had been watching orange-crowned and blackpoll warblers and pointed them out to us. Including those last two, we ended the day with thirty-four species of warblers sighted, lacking only the mourning and Connecticut, and a grand total of almost 140 species of birds.

Milkweeds are coming into bloom along rural roadsides, and their sweet fragrance clings to the warm evening air. Few wildflowers can match the rich aroma of the common milkweed, a blend of lilac, trailing arbutus, and honeysuckle.

Insects are attracted to the flowers of the milkweed. This morning I checked a patch of the three-foot-high plants growing in our orchard. The clusters of lavender florets were covered with a variety of insects: a great spangled fritillary butterfly was sipping nectar, as were honeybees, paper wasps, skeletonizer moths, and numerous species of flies. Orange milkweed bugs and several monarch butterfly larvae were feeding on the plants as well.

Milkweeds are so named for the thick milky juice, something like Elmer's glue, that bleeds from stems and leaves when they are broken. The monarch larva feeds on the sticky and bitter juice, which may explain why predators seldom feed on the adult butterfly: they must taste awful. The nectar, though, makes excellent honey.

In contrast, the bright-orange butterfly weed, which also is in bloom now, is not milky when broken. Maybe that is why monarch larvae are seldom seen feeding on this member of the milkweed family, though the adult butterflies love its nectar.

Butterfly weed is rare in this part of the country—I have found only one of the handsome plants growing in the wild hereabouts—but it is common farther west. We have started butterfly weeds from seed and now have them growing in our garden and a few along the roadsides.

Swamp milkweed, as its name suggests, grows in swamps and wet areas. Its flowers are a delicate dusty rose, though not as aromatic as those of the common milkweed. This plant, too, is a common host to monarch larvae.

Last summer we had some monarch caterpillars on a milkweed bouquet in the house. As the growing larvae consumed the leaves, we would bring in new plants, mostly swamp milkweed. Unbeknownst to us, the new plants had freshly laid monarch eggs on them, which soon hatched as minute caterpillars. Barely an eighth of an inch long, the tiny caterpillars already had the black-with-white-and-yellow bands of their larger cousins feeding nearby. At one point there were nine monarch caterpillars of various sizes feeding on our milkweed bouquet.

Other interesting and pretty, though less fragrant, wildflowers are blooming along roadsides right now. One is chicory, whose inch-across flowers are as blue as the July sky. I have long admired chicory for its ability to thrive in the harsh habitat of road edges, oftentimes growing right in the gravel.

Chicory is an immigrant; it was brought from Europe as a cultivated plant. Like the dandelion, though, it jumped the garden fence and turned wild. In parts of Europe the dried roots of chicory were used as a substitute for coffee. Even today coffee can be bought that is "mellowed with chicory." The sky-blue flowers of chicory are at their brightest early in the forenoon; in this sweltering ninety-degree heat, however, the flowers are closed by noon. Very smart.

Also blooming on road banks now is the yellow evening primrose. The four-petaled flowers blossom from the top of the plant, which may grow to be four feet tall by the end of summer.

Even taller than the primroses are the towering stalks of

common mullein, whose small yellow flowers bloom on a clublike flower head at the top of the plant. Common mullein may grow to be six feet tall. Mixed in with the mulleins and primroses are a few yellow goat's-beards. The goat's-beard, like the chicory, closes its blossoms at noon.

Adding a touch of white to the roadsides is Queen Anne's lace. The flat clusters of lacy flowers are nice along roads but not in tilled fields. I pull them out with a passion in my hay fields. To many farmers, Queen Anne's lace is merely a wild carrot and a curse.

Soon the roadside will become even richer in color as joe-pye weed and other summer flowers burst into bloom. But not richer in fragrance than now, with the milkweeds. Just ask any bee.

COYOTE

Until a few years ago I had never heard a coyote. When our children were small they played with a toy where they would turn a pointer on a large clocklike dial to an animal, pull a cord, and the animal would cackle, bark, moo, or whatever. One animal was the coyote. When the cord was pulled a husky masculine voice said, "THIS IS THE COYOTE"; then a series of weak, scratchy yaps and barks issued forth from the plastic contraption. I must confess, Fisher-Price did not prepare me for the real thing.

We were camped high in the middle of nowhere when around midnight we were startled from sleep by a wailing and yapping and crying the likes of which I had never heard in my life. A whisper from the next tent announced: COYOTES. For maybe ten minutes we listened to the wild, wondrous serenade that seemed to come from just outside our campsite. Then as suddenly as the coyotes had begun, they fell silent. I guessed there must have been at least a dozen of the ghostly minstrels, but my friend, who was familiar with the ways of coyote, said there were no more than two.

In the past few weeks we have discovered that coyotes have become our neighbors. Two were seen during the week of deer season within a mile of our farm. For a number of years there have been occasional reports of coyote sightings, but never this close. The news is always met with mixed feelings. Some welcome the animals with the attitude that if westerners can live with the crafty critters, so can we. Others say that the coyote is not filling a void in the local environment but will be displacing other, native predators like the red fox.

The origin of our Ohio coyotes is something of a mystery. Did they move in from the West or from the East? The Ohio coyote is one of the biggest in the nation, with the males weighing as much as fifty pounds; the typical western male, in contrast, may weigh only thirty pounds. Another difference is that the western coyote is much more vocal, a real song-dog. Every night their voices can be heard ringing from desert and prairie, and from the rim of the high plateau. Eastern coyotes rarely sing, and when they do it usually is during the winter when they form pair bonds.

A biologist once kept track of a family of coyotes that spent the winter under the floor of an abandoned house. The only time those coyotes opened their mouths was to eat and pant. There was no singing at all.

If our coyotes are of the eastern race, they came by way of Canada and New England. Moving east from the Upper Great Lakes region, their ancestors mixed genes with a remnant race of timber wolves in southern Ontario. (As long as there were healthy populations of wolves in the East, their strong social orders had kept the coyotes out.) By the 1940s and 1950s the coyotes had become well established in New England. Crossing with timber wolves increased the coyotes' size and gave them the sense to keep their singing to a minimum—a must to survive in the populous East. Throughout the next several decades the eastern coyote kept spreading west and south, through the Appalachians, and in time reached Ohio.

If, however, our neighbor coyotes are of the western race, they simply came loping in through the midwestern states and, according to some outdoorsmen, thrived on the abundance of our wild and agricultural fare, gained twenty pounds, and for some strange reason lost their voice. Maybe they ate green persimmons.

In fact, coyotes *will* eat just about anything they come across: voles, mice, muskrats, poodles, rabbits, grouse, pheasants, turkeys, ducks, and songbirds. They also eat berries, nuts, frogs, and snakes—and, of course, sheep and lambs. Since Ohio produces more sheep than any other state east of the Mississippi, coyotes are a threat to those farmers. Our neighbor used to raise some sheep, and to promote his product he stuck a decal on his wagon: "Eat American Lamb: Ten Million Coyotes Can't Be Wrong."

I admire wily coyote and his amazing ability to survive and thrive against tremendous odds. I just hope his arrival will not greatly upset the ecological balance of our wild communities.

SELBORNE

Last December I received a book and letter from a friend in England. Our milk hauler delivered the book, by way of a farmer and friend near Walnut Creek to whom the package had been mailed. It's a long story, so I won't go into much detail. But I do want to let Mr. Shaylor tell part of the story. He wrote:

"This year I was asked by a friend if I could supply cattle to graze some fields at a village called Selborne some 10 miles from us. I took 15 of our beef heifers, mostly Belgian blue and Piemontaise crosses out of British Friesians.

"I was aware that the village was an important focus for naturalists and conservationists and people came from all over the world to visit the village and walk up the big hill where our cattle have been grazing and so I called into the museum to try to learn some more. I saw Gilbert White's book and immediately thought of my friends the Millers and yourself. In fact I haven't had time to read the book yet so I hope it is of interest to you."

It is of interest to me. Indeed it is.

The book is called *The Natural History of Selborne*. It was published in 1788 but dated 1789, as was the practice then to give books an extra year of "newness." What is so remarkable about *Selborne* is that it has been in continuous print since— somewhere between two and three hundred editions and translations! Next to Izaak Walton's *Compleat Angler, Selborne* is the most frequently published volume of natural history and fourth most frequently published book in the English language.

Gilbert White was born in 1720 in Selborne, a village in Hampshire, fifty miles southwest of London. Educated at Oxford, he did some traveling on horseback, including a visit to Stonehenge, but eventually returned along the deep-cut cartways to Selborne and his grandfather's home, "The Wakes."

White was an ordained Anglican clergyman but never attained the position of vicar held by his grandfather, remaining a curate throughout his ministering life. He was sort of a rural vicar. He also was a lifelong bachelor.

Soon after returning to Selborne and the family estate, Reverend White began keeping notes on natural happenings. On January 12, 1768, for example, he wrote: "A cock-pheasant appeared on the dunghill at the end of the stable; tamed by hunger." By March the cucumber fruits were swelling and the rooks incubating eggs.

The book *Selborne,* however, is a collection of 110 longer, descriptive, anecdotal letters that White wrote to two friends, Thomas Pennant and Daines Barrington, over a twenty-year period. White had saved copies of his letters, and when the book was compiled, any gaps were filled with new sections disguised as letters.

Publishing *Selborne* as a collection of letters also preserved White's modesty because, after all, Selborne was a village of the common man, a "single straggling street through a sheltered vale." Here is a typical passage, from Letter 11 to Thomas Pennant: "Bats drink on the wing, like swallows, by sipping the surface, as they play over pools and streams. They love to frequent waters, not only for the sake of drinking, but on the account of insects, which are found over them in the greatest plenty."

White believed: "All nature is so full, that that district produces the greatest variety which is the most examined." Seventy years later Henry David Thoreau, who revered *Selborne* over almost all other books of science, wrote: " . . . A man must see, before he can say."

Even though I had often read about Gilbert White and *The Natural History of Selborne*, I had never seen the book until the milk hauler brought me the gift sent from England.

Thank you, David Shaylor.

COMMUNITY

It has been said that community is like an old coat—you aren't aware of it until it is taken away. I became aware of what community is when I was drafted during the Vietnam War and served two years working in a hospital in a big city. My comfortable coat of community was taken away. But that is getting ahead of my story.

It is often said that a man standing in his own field is unable to see it. I think that was the case with me growing up: I had my nose too close to the picture.

That changed somewhat when I was about twelve years old. During the Eisenhower presidency and the USDA's Soil Bank days, the government told the farmers how many acres of wheat they could grow.

In order to verify farmer compliance, the government sent a technician out to measure the field. If there was too much wheat, it had to be cut for hay or ensiled. When the young technician visited our farm he had a large aerial photograph of the entire neighborhood, which he spread out on the hood of his car. Dad then showed him which field was sown in wheat.

I looked at the map and marveled at the landscape from the air: the view the red-tailed hawk had when it soared high over the fields. There, meandering through the pasture field, was the creek where we fished and swam. And the woods with all its interesting creatures. There was the one-room schoolhouse with its massive white oak by the front entrance and the red oak next to the baseball backstop. I could already smell the freshly oiled wood floor and felt myself looking forward with anticipation to September when the new school year would begin. It was there on those three acres, after all, that the study of nature and creation and language and music and arithmetic and softball became one.

From that photograph my horizons broadened. But it was when I moved to the city to start my Vietnam War conscientious objector service that I began to realize what community is really all about.

I started work in November, and within a month it snowed. Going to my landlady's garage, I found a snow shovel and started cleaning off her sidewalk along the street. Ah, this was more farmwork again, hands-on labor! I got carried away and shoveled off the snow several houses down and up the street. When I returned to the house, my landlady was extremely upset.

"What?" I asked.

"You cleaned off Mrs. —'s sidewalk . . . and I don't like her!"

I wised up in a hurry. Not only did the people dress differently in the city, they thought differently, too.

When I had left the farm for the city, I thought I might not return. Maybe I would gravitate toward a higher-tech life. But I did return to the farm, where, as Bill McKibben writes, "humus and human meet." Where, instead of Peyton Place, I watched orioles and butterflies and listened to what the land had to teach.

I returned to a community that choose to work with their hands, believing manual labor is close to godliness. A community where technology is restricted and "book learning" is frowned upon. Where even the hymns are passed on without the notes being written down. In this culture, you learn from a master. There is always someone who possesses the arts and skills you need.

I soon noticed on returning home that my role models were local people, neighbors instead of entertainment celebrities. My uncle, who lived on the next farm and was a voracious reader, enthralled me with dog stories— "The Little Shepherd of Kingdom Come" and "The Voice of Bugle Ann."

Another neighbor, a fine horseman, taught me a great deal about handling and loving the gentle draft horse. When he lost his larynx to cancer (no, he didn't smoke), his horses responded to his slightest touch of the lines and he continued to farm.

Most of these role models are now resting in hillside cemeteries on farms throughout the neighborhood. I often hear that our people came to America (on the invitation of the Quaker William Penn) for religious freedom. That is true, but they also came to have their own farms. Practically all of the first settlers are buried on the land they tilled—on the land that nurtured them and their families.

Of course, the fact that we stayed with horse farming and animal traction when the rest of society switched to fossil fuel traction didn't go unnoticed by us younger boys. We had never heard of Ned Ludd, and we would say to our father, "Dad, if we would get rid of these horses we could milk ten more cows."

His response was always the same: "But then we wouldn't have all that good horse manure, and besides, tractors compact the soil."

If we Amish in northeastern Ohio look at our community and all its small villages—Berlin, Mt. Hope, Charm, Farmerstown, Fredericksburg, Kidron—that are thriving in spite of a

Wal-Mart ten miles away, we can see it is because of the horse. Seldom do we travel farther than five or six miles to do our business. Some may go to Wal-Mart, but not on a weekly basis. The standardbred horse helps us, even if we think globally, to act locally.

These small towns and their markets benefit the outlying counties. A while back I took some eggs to the weekly auction in Mt. Hope. As I carried them in I noticed a car with its trunk open and an elderly farmer lifting out a case of eggs. The license plate was from several counties west of us. Why, I thought, do they have to bring their eggs all this way to flood our market?

Then I realized that their small towns and markets are gone, and my heart softened.

Welcome friend, we are delighted to have you here.

SHARING WORK WITH CHILDREN

A minister friend of mine once told me that parents often change their views on child-raising when their children become teenagers. "Before those years," he said, "we often have all, or at least most, of the answers for nurturing and training children. Even to the point of being arrogant about it. Teenagers bring us back to reality." I consider him not only a wise but also an honest man.

So before I venture any farther down this treacherous path, I will make a disclaimer: This is not a "how-to" piece, but rather one on the pleasures of working together with children—your own and your neighbors'. It is about children and adults working together for a common good. I see it everywhere in the neighborhood.

Since we live on a farm, our children, once they reached an age when they could help with the work, have always played an essential role in our livelihood. They help us make things happen. They make farming more pleasurable. Here we share in the pleasures of planting and the joys of harvest, become a part of the unfolding of the seasons, watch the cycle of life and death, agonize over the scarcity of rain in drought years, and understand together why the occasional Friday-night pizza delivery was suspended because of a dearth of income.

This working together as a family is likely one of the primary reasons our people traditionally have preferred an agrarian way of life. On a farm, children early on can be given tasks at which they feel they can succeed, and then do. Such as feeding calves: they watch the calf grow into a heifer and then have a calf of its own, which enters the milking herd. A lesson in economics. Having several rabbits to care for also teaches economics (it's quite profitable when Dad furnishes the feed) and the facts of reproduction.

As soon as our children were old enough, they were given the task of naming the newborn calves. And what a delightful array of names our cows now have. Children are far more creative than their parents at such things. Thus we have Fudge, Lobb, Rubena, Iris, and Petunia, along with the more traditional Doris, Bonnie, and Patsy. One requirement is that the calf's name must begin with the same letter as its mother's name. The other day Patsy had a heifer calf, and it was named Pepsi. Who knows, maybe next year she will have a Pizza.

Another of the pleasures of traditional farming is working together with your neighbors' children while threshing. Usually at around the age of ten to twelve, boys, and girls if needed, begin to help out with that job. That is, they help in the fields to stack the sheaves of grain on the wagons. Here the art of correctly loading the bundles—heads inward, knots down, butts out a bit from the wagon's edge, the center filled but not too full, watch out for thistles—is taught by older brothers or sisters, fathers or neighbors.

If the wagons are correctly loaded, they can bounce along our hillsides without a bundle being lost. I enjoy the look of appreciation on the radiant faces of the loaders as they watch a wagon depart for the barn. Then one remarks, "Now, that's a nice load."

Soon the talk switches to what's for dinner: meatloaf or fried chicken? Surely mashed potatoes and gravy. Ah, maybe there will be pineapple rings, a special treat for the youngsters with a sweet tooth. The girls who help with the threshing eat at the table with the crew and are excused from helping with the meal or washing dishes. They sit in the shade until it's time to go back to the field. They love it.

In a year or two the boys begin to fork the sheaves of grain onto the wagons. It's sort of a rite of passage: the Amish bar mitzvah. From here on the boys also may take the team and wagon, a job that brings the added responsibility of driving the team and loaded wagon into the barn without scraping the drive belt, and then forking the bundles into the threshing machine. The teamster unloads from the front of the wagon and always pitches to the upper inside of the feeder, never one bundle on top of another. And hang on to the fork! Forks inside a threshing machine make a lot of noise and do no good.

Silo filling is mostly done by boys over sixteen and men because of the hard physical labor involved in loading the heavy bundles of corn. Still, there can be considerable interaction with the children. Several years ago we were filling silo at a neighbor's farm; the family's daughter, who was maybe ten at the time, offered to help drive my team while I loaded the wagon. We talked about school, which had just started for the year, her favorite subjects and teachers, her friends, their pony. We had an enjoyable day. Now whenever I see her she has a wonderful smile for me because we remember that day of filling silo.

The following week at the next farm, the neighbor's five-year-old son volunteered to help me drive the team. We've been friends ever since. Although doing fun things with children can build a closeness and is important, doing work together seems to build mutual respect. Respect cannot be demanded; it must be earned. For some reason, heaving and shoving together does the trick.

It is when we're mucking out our horse stables that our seventeen-year-old son, who seems to have had more than his share of angst-ridden years concerning plain living, and I have our best discussions. There is something about that strenuous work—maybe it's the aroma—that melts away communication barriers. Our stable definitely wasn't designed for ease of cleanout. There are six stalls side by side, with the manure spreader parked at one end, so by the time we get to the stalls at the far end we're doing more walking than anything else. But it makes for good talking. And we're approaching the time when we'll switch forks—my eight-tiner for his five-tiner.

It is here in the stable where I think I see subtle signs that he shares his parents' view that "a man is rich in proportion to the things he can afford to leave alone." As I reach out and put my hand on his shoulder, I say, "Son, if at times you forget the admonishing I've done and advice I've given over the years, don't forget the good talks we've had in this stable. But above all else, please remember that your mother and I love you very much."

THE VALUE OF LOVE

Farming has fallen on tough times, especially the small-scale, diversified, noncontract livestock farms the Amish in this part of the country (Homes County, Ohio) prefer. Hog prices recently hit a thirty-year low; cull cow prices are scraping bottom; and milk prices, the mainstay of the community, are down as well. Our neighbor told me that for his July milk he received the lowest prices in thirteen years.

One benefit, however, of these depressed farm prices is that I have become even more keenly aware of how important the help of my neighbors is in making farming profitable. I refer here to that exchange of labor where no money is involved. I never carry my wallet or checkbook when working on neighboring farms because I'm always paying back with my labor what they have already done, or will do, for me.

This moneyless exchange often involves more than labor. It can be a sharing of machinery and knowledge, or even of fertility. One year we had more third-cutting hay than we needed; the field was almost too far away to graze, so we made a deal with our neighbor who was in need of more hay. He got the six acres of hay—probably around two hundred bales—and in turn he spread six loads of manure on the field and we got a free service from his draft horse stud.

In our neighborhood exchange of labor we never keep close track of the hours we trade. Accounting usually goes by a half-day or a full day's work. Last fall, for instance, I helped one neighbor run his shocks of corn through the mechanical corn husker and shredder. So he still owes me a day of labor, which will be to help me put up a new line fence. We both know that good fences make good neighbors. Besides, he has a power posthole digger that we will use to bore the holes for the new posts. So when the cost of his equipment is figured in, he will be doing more for me than I did for him with my manual labor. But I know that when we're finished with the fence, and we both look at it with satisfaction, he'll insist that we are now "fair and square."

A lot of this exchange is tied to the biblical injunctions to "love thy neighbor as thyself" and "do unto others as you would have them do unto you." And to the belief that your neighbor is your neighbor whether he attends your church or is a nonbeliever. So I help him and he helps me. We need each other.

This love for your neighbor was clearly pointed out to me a few years ago when an elderly farmer from our community died. His family lived at the far end of our local school district, and his wish was to be buried in the neighborhood cemetery instead of the cemetery of their church district. He said he wants to be with the people he spent most of his time with: his neighbors who with their labor made it possible for him to farm in a low-cost way, the people who were always there when he needed them, and with whom he laughed and hunted and shared wonderful meals. Of course, he was a generous man and helped his neighbors much in return.

What does this free labor mean to us farmers economically? Probably much more than we realize because we are so used to it. For one thing, I know it enables us to harvest our crops with a minimal amount of machinery and fossil fuel use.

This summer we had an answer to that question, in a small way. In our real horse–powered agriculture, oats are still an important crop—first as horse feed, then as hog and chicken feed, and finally for the dairy cows. And in the winter we eat rolled oats for breakfast.

In any case, when a severe summer storm threatens, especially around mid-June when the oats are "heading out" and at their most vulnerable for lodging, our first thought is "Oh no, the oats!" This past summer was an anxious one. Our field endured four major thunderstorms—from all four directions. The first, from the east, also had hail. By the time the fourth one, from the west, was finished, our oats—and our hopes—were flattened.

The crop was beyond cutting with a binder, so we hired a custom operator with his combine to harvest the oats. For ten acres it cost $225. And then the grain was too wet to store, so we had to hire someone to dry it. Another $180. In a storm-free year the crop would have been harvested with the free labor of my neighbors and $10 worth of fuel. As the saying goes, "What we don't spend is profit."

There is also a saving of money beyond the direct exchange of labor, and that is in multi-use equipment. This week the last silo in our silo-filling ring was filled. The Weavers had planted some corn late, and it wasn't ready to be ensiled until the end of September, which is late here. Seven wagons and seven men worked together picking up the bundles of corn. The wagons and teams are the same ones we use for hay making, threshing, wood and apple hauling, taking the schoolchildren from one school to another for a game of softball on pleasant fall afternoons, and dozens of other jobs around the farm. No special or expensive equipment is needed to fill our silos.

Most of us do possess our own silo filler, an archaic machine that is fairly inexpensive and not cumbersome to store, plus a corn binder, a 1940s machine that cuts the corn and ties it (most of the time) into bundles. The binder is also used to cut dried-down corn when its fodder is needed for the livestock's winter bedding. So it, too, is not a single-purpose machine.

Seven wagons and teamsters, each picking up bundles of corn and loading them on the wagons in this perfect weather of September, when the crispness of the early morning kept our coats on for the first load: this was labor exchange at its finest. Conditions were so ideal that not to feel good about the work would have been impossible.

As the sun warmed the morning air, coats were thrown aside. Overhead, migrating turkey vultures and red-tailed hawks began leaning into nothingness, searching for the rising updrafts to ride the invisible towers of heated air into the cobalt autumn sky. Monarch butterflies drifted southwest on their long journey to the Sierra Madre in Mexico. Blue jays scolded. Crows called.

For a month, since filling the first silo in late August, we had been working together. Not every day, of course, but about two days each week. This last day the Percheron teams outnumbered the Belgians, for the farm was along the township road that the draft horse people affectionately call "Percheron Alley." The mood of the crew was lively; talk flowed freely in the field and even more so around the dinner table as the farm economy—the low milk prices, the slow rebound of hog prices—was discussed. Best of all were the stories: stories, some tragic, some humorous, that are retold annually.

But this exchange of labor is more than monetary; I detected as much at that dinner table. It is also about the good feeling of helping your neighbor. It reminds me of a river— serene and beautiful, yet within its gentle flow is great strength. Still, that power is not a controlling force; it is peaceful and satisfying. There is a special sort of security in working beyond the grips of the money economy.

As I unloaded the last load and looked out across the fertile valley, over the crowns of the creekside cottonwoods and willows, at the farms we worked on during this past month, and at our farm in the distance, I sighed with gratitude for the blessings of living in a neighborhood where sharing labor is a work of love.